A PARENT'S GUIDE TO PAINTBALL

STEVE DAVIDSON

A Parent's Guide to Paintball
Steve Davidson

ISBN -10 1894953-584
ISBN -13 978-1894953-580

Liaison Press
Published in Canada
Vancouver, British Columbia, Canada

A Parent's Guide to Paintball

Steve Davidson

LIAISON PRESS
VANCOUVER | CANADA

Contents

To my wife, Karen Lynn for being perhaps the only person on the entire globe who truly understands me.

ACKNOWLEDGEMENTS

This is the part of the book where I thank all of the people who were instrumental in either making it happen, providing support or both. As usual, there are far too many individuals to mention individually, so I will issue a blanket 'thank you' to all of the players, field owners, event promoters, teammates and industry personalities who—whether they knew it or not—have contributed to my knowledge and understanding of this game for the past quarter century. Several people are, however, deserving of special mention. Pete Allen for his early support, encouragement and editorial skills, Anne Stickle for her copyediting skills (and speed!), Biff Thiele—one of the unacknowledged fathers of paintball and the team at Kee Action Sports who made this project their own—George, Jason, Jason and Joe.

I would also like to personally thank each and every paintballer around the world who has taken the time to introduce someone to the game and who has presented the sport in a positive manner.

INTRODUCTION

I have prepared this book for the millions of parents out there whose children either play paintball or have expressed a desire to do so. Young and old, male and female, rich and poor, athlete and couch potato, honor roll student and dropout—chances are they have played, want to play, or have friends who do.

Dozens of publications and hundreds, if not thousands, of websites are devoted to paintball and every aspect of it, all designed to accomplish two goals: getting your child to play paintball and getting your pride and joy to spend money on paintball. None of them are suited to answering the real questions parents ask about any unfamiliar activity their child might want to become involved with, like: Is it really safe? Who are the people my child will be influenced by? How much will it really cost *me*? Should I get involved? Is this just a kid's thing? And so on.

In other words, no definitive resource for parents explains what paintball is all about…until now.

Such a book being presented by a paintball veteran might give you pause, but I assure you I have pulled no punches when it comes to portraying the darker aspects of this game and industry. There is much to be admired about paintball and many positive aspects to it. But, like any other human activity, there can be some bad mixed in with the good.

I believe every parent has the right to guide, teach, mentor, and educate their children in the manner they feel appropriate. My providing parents with this resource will help enable informed decisions regarding their child and the game of paintball. Parents presented with my truthful, unvarnished information on this game should thus be able to make positive decisions for both themselves and their children.

And I believe that, given the correct information, most parents will not only want to see their child involved with this fun sport, but may even decide to join them!

More information is available on our supporting website: http://paintballparentsguide.com.

ABOUT THE ADVERTISERS IN THIS BOOK

Numerous paintball companies have chosen to support the publication of this book in the form of the advertisements that you see in the various chapters and sections. Each of these companies has made a long-term commitment to the paintball industry and its players. They are all fine, upstanding members of the paintball community who have earned the trust and respect of players and their peers.

These companies have chosen to support this book because they endorse the concepts of family-oriented play, giving something back to their community, providing information and promoting safe-play practices.

None of these companies contributed to the content of the book, nor were any of them involved in the editorial process. The process of putting this book together was specifically designed to separate the writing process and the marketing process so that readers can be assured that the contents are free of commercial interests.

With that said, I greatly appreciate their support in helping to bring this book to you and hope that you, the reader, will consider patronizing them in a manner that is consistent with the recommendations and advice you will find here.

CHAPTER 1:
AN INTRODUCTION TO PAINTBALL

PAINTBALL'S HISTORY

Numerous myths surround the invention of paintball. It's probably true that just about any kid growing up during the 50s and 60s thought that it would be a great thing to be able to shoot some kind of *real* bullets out of their toy army guns.

Lots of us did, in fact, do just that. Remember the admonition that if you play with a BB gun, "you'll put your eye out with that thing!"? (This is precisely the reason why I had to borrow a friend's gun when I wanted to play BB gun and dirt bomb wars.) Who can blame parents' reluctance to let their children play with toys that can cause permanent injury?

In the late 1970s, the Nelson Paint Company developed a gas-operated gun and *marking pellets* for a variety of industries, including Forestry and Ranching. The guns and pellets were used variously to mark trees for removal, cows to be culled from the herd, and essentially anything else that required putting a semi-permanent mark on an object from a distance.

Given that the folks using these guns were normal American outdoor types, it probably took less than thirty seconds from opening the package to the first cowboy-on-cowboy paintball war. Whoever was involved in that encounter can lay legitimate claim to having played the first "paintball" game.

The official history of the game (which can be found in numerous incarnations on the Internet and in the various books written about the sport) begins with two friends, Charles Gaines and Bill Guernsey. The story goes that they were discussing the advantages and disadvantages of different types of survival skills (city survival versus outdoor survival).

They concluded that they needed something, like a marking gun and a set of rules, that would allow people to test their individual skills against each other. After about a year of searching, Gaines and Guernsey chose the Nelson Paint company's guns and pellets, developed a set of rules for "survival games," and invited 12 friends out to the woods of Henniker, New Hampshire in June of 1981 to test out their new creation.

The version of the game played back then was every man for himself—quite unlike today's team sport. Interestingly enough, the winning player (Richie White) won without firing a single shot—he just snuck around the woods, displaying his ultimate hunter skills and out-foxed all of the other players.

Shortly after this experimental game, the inventors created a company called The National Survival Game to market the sport as a franchise. Several playing fields still in existence today started out as NSG franchise fields—but unfortunately for the founders of the game, many other would-be field owners felt that their fees were too high and it wasn't long before several independent operations had opened up for business.

In 1982, NSG decided it would be a good idea to have their fields host local competitions that would lead to a National Tournament Championship, creating what has now become the high-end of the sport—tournament paintball.

A few years later, several fields across the country hosted what were then termed Big Games—the objective of which was to have as many people as possible playing at once. Shortly thereafter, the concept of the Scenario Game was born—events which have a theme and encourage players to role-play within it. (William Shatner, the actor of Star Trek and TJ Hooker fame, has popularized scenario games as annual charity events, the first of which had a Star Trek theme, pitting the Federation, the Klingons and the Borg against each other.)

By the mid-80's, virtually every manner of paintball play

had been invented, and it was only a question of growing the sport and gaining wider appeal.

By the beginning of the nineties, paintball was well on its way to becoming a pastime enjoyed by millions around the world.

The sport is now recognized by the Sporting Goods Manufacturers Association, whose marketing surveys reveal that it is a billion-dollar industry, played by over 15 million people every year in the United States alone.

Paintball now graces newsstands with numerous publications, is one of the largest E-Bay sporting goods categories and even has several television shows broadcast nationally on a weekly basis.

From playing "army" in the woods, paintball has now become a common, everyday activity, enjoyed by millions from all walks of life.

PAINTBALL'S HISTORICAL TIME-LINE
1981: First game played (Henniker, New Hampshire)
1982: First national competition played
1986: First national publication out on newsstands
1990: First publicly-traded paintball company established
1992: First National Tournament League founded (NPPL)
1996: First Nationally-Televised Competition (ESPN)
1999: First Recognized as a Legitimate Sport by SGMA
2000: First National Collegiate Event

WHO ARE THE PAINTBALL PLAYERS?

Literally, anyone.

Let's back up a second and look at this from a parent's point of view.

If you are questioning whether your child should be allowed to play or not—only you can decide.

If, on the other hand, you are looking for examples to help you make that decision, here is some information for you.

I have personally seen children as young as 6 and people as old as 86 playing paintball. I've played with and against:

- Kids (6 to 17)
- Women and girls
- Men and boys
- Several players missing legs
- Several players who are deaf
- Several players who are in wheelchairs
- People from—Germany, France, Canada, Japan, Thailand, Russia, Czechoslovakia, Israel, Spain, Brazil, England, Ireland, Korea.
- Police officers, firemen, attorneys, day workers, students, NASA scientists, janitors, Active Duty Military, doctors, nurses, accountants, salesmen.

Among all of those disparate groups, I've only found one major question when it comes to whether someone should play or not and that question is: can they handle competitive play?

Maturity does not have an age limit. I've seen so-called adults act in a completely childish manner. I've seen 6- year-olds exhibit conduct and sportsmanship way beyond what anyone would normally think possible.

On its record, paintball has proven to be a tremendous equalizer in terms of game play. The paintball marker serves to remove gross differences in strength, speed and agility, offering a game in which a 6-year-old *can* compete effectively against a 30-year-old (not to mention allowing a 30-year-old to play effectively against an 86-year-old).

Conclusion: Anyone who wants to play paintball can. So long as they are armed with the correct information, evaluate their own desire, review their abilities and make an informed decision, playing paintball is just like any other fun physical

activity.

When making that decision for others—as parents ought to do for their children—it's important to separate your own feelings, hot buttons and prejudices from those of your child's. It is also important to remember that paintball is only a game. As such, it stands for nothing, teaches nothing, advocates nothing; it takes no political positions, confers no lifestyle, imposes no moral boundaries—except for those that you choose to pass along to your child.

A strong parent, one who has taught and continues to teach good, strong values to their child, one who stays involved, who encourages and supports their child, will find that paintball offers an excellent tool for reinforcing many of life's important lessons, such as: fair play, following rules, teamwork, leadership, planning, friendship, responsibility, and much more.

WHAT IS A TYPICAL GAME LIKE?

A playing field is laid out, either in an area of woods or on an open field with man-made obstacles (the area usually being several hundred feet long by a few hundred feet wide). Starting locations for two teams are designated—referred to as *flag stations*—and the teams are chosen, usually by dividing the number of available players in half.

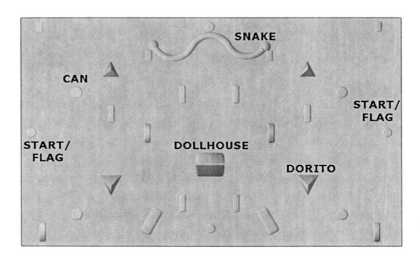

Figure 1. A typical National Professional Paintball League—NPPL—field. This field is 180 feet long by 100 feet wide. The starting locations are shown (Start/Flag) and several unique styles of inflatable obstacles called bunkers *are labeled. Most bunkers range between 2 and 10 feet high or long.*

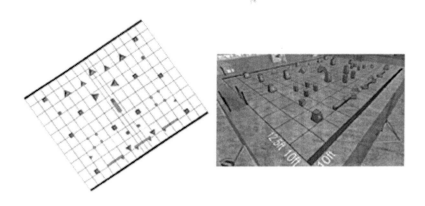

Figure 2. *A Paintball Sports Promotions event field, shown in diagrammatic and 3D images. Field layouts for national competition are usually distributed over the Internet several weeks before an event so that teams can practice prior to attending.*

Figure 3. A scenario game or theme *field, this one replicating a town. This and several other themed fields can be found at the Skirmish USA facility.*

Figure *4. Another themed field—the Castle at EMR paintball.*

Figure 5. A woodsball field with the addition of man-made bunkers. (From the Invasion of Normandy scenario game at Skirmish USA)

The two teams occupy their flag stations and, on a signal, (an airhorn, a whistle, or simply a shouted "Game on!") the game begins. Some players begin shooting almost immediately in order to deny their opponents maneuvering lanes or particular locations on the field. Other players run and slide into key positions and then begin to fire themselves.

Following *the break* (the opening few seconds of a game), things settle down into a battle of fire and maneuver. Each team tries to eliminate opposing players by hitting them with a paintball, either by maneuvering into advantageous positions, winning a *snap shooting* duel or *shutting them down* by flooding their positions with so many paintballs that they can't leave their cover to look, shoot or move.

The objective in most games is to capture a flag—either a flag in the middle of the field (called "center flag games," usually for smaller teams), or a flag in their opponent's flag station (called "dual flag games"). Once a non-eliminated player has taken a flag, it must be placed in the opponent's flag station (for center flag games) or in their own flag station (for dual flag games).

When played on a *concept field* (one with artificial terrain), games are usually very quick (1 to 5 minutes in duration), very intense, fast and loud (because good players communicate all the time). Games played in the woods are usually slower paced, involve more maneuvering and less shooting, and generally last longer (5 to 15 minutes or more).

During scenario games, play lasts for 12 to 24 hours, usually with a break during the middle of the night. Unlike other game formats, scenario games allow players that have been eliminated to re-enter the game at set intervals.

The game is still the same, regardless of the type of field; players seek to mark an opponent, eliminating them from the game, so that they can then go on to achieve the major objective of capturing a flag.

IS PAINTBALL LEGITIMATE?

If I were writing this section twenty years from now, I wouldn't need to be writing it, since paintball would have nearly half a century of existence behind it. We're only a quarter of a century into its development though, so it's probably necessary that I provide you with a little more background on this crazy thing called paintball.

When I first started playing this game, it took me over a year of hunting to find a location where I could participate; no one I knew—co-workers, friends, family, acquaintances, people on the street—had ever heard of it. Most of those I asked thought I was some kind of neo-Nazi, gun-nut survivalist for even being interested.

For the first several years of my playing career, the "wannabe-survivalist" perception was the world's perception of the game. This anti-paintball viewpoint was so prevalent and problematic that we all did as much as we could do, both personally and within the industry, to divorce ourselves from the military image.

Player uniforms became more colorful. Fields moved from the woods into open arenas. Paintball guns became known as paintball *markers*. Everyone was drilled on how to respond to news reporters' negatively-oriented questions. Every player became a goodwill ambassador for the sport, explaining to anyone who would listen for half a second that it was a sport, not military training.

In some respects, our response to the world at large could be seen as polishing or political correctness; the paintball marker is still a gun under the strict definition of the word (a device for firing a projectile), we still engage in what is essentially warfare, the skills we learn are similar to those necessary to surviving in a hostile environment, and the training we use draws much of its methodology from the military.

However, we have achieved our goal of casting paintball in a positive light. If there had not been any truth to our contentions, what we were saying would never have caught hold.

Ultimately, it all comes down to how *you* wish to perceive the game. You can call a marker a gun, using the word as an epithet and dragging in all of the negativity that goes with the subject, drowning out all of the distinctions that separate a gun (a device for firing a projectile) from a firearm (a device utilizing combustion to fire a projectile), or you can call it a marker (a device for firing a paintball projectile) and react to it for what it is: a tool for playing a game, devoid of any political or moral positions, an inert object that only stands for what you decide it should stand for.

As for the legitimacy of the game: a billion dollars a year in sales, 20+million people playing in the United States, the export of the game to virtually every country around the globe, a best-selling video game (Greg Hastings' *Tournament Paintball* (and its sequels), the creation of municipal paintball fields, the founding of a national college league and the borrowing of paintball technology by the NASA/AMES Jet Propulsion Laboratory pretty much speak for themselves.

COMMON PAINTBALL MYTHS

1. **Paintball is competition and competition is *bad*.**

This is not a myth—except for its conclusion. Competition in and of itself is one of the major facets of life. We all compete, constantly, for everything—jobs, mates, parking spaces, positions within our communities—everything. A fact of life is neither good nor bad. Instead, we need to focus on the lessons competition teaches us; it is here where paintball shines. The results and effects of competition on the paintball field are immediate: you eliminated someone or they eliminated you. Your team won the game or it lost the game. You didn't do something you should have, and a teammate got eliminated.

The lessons learned are immediate also. Analyzing results and applying them teaches players how to deal with the consequences of their actions and the actions of those around them. Learning how to deal properly with success and failure are among life's greatest lessons. Learning those lessons can never be bad.

2. Paintball uses a gun (firearm) and guns are *bad*.

As was said earlier, there is a distinction between a gun and a firearm. Firearms are devices which have drawn all of the acrimonious political debate—one we will not enter into here, since a person's view on the subject is unlikely to change no matter what I say. The people who take this position believe all guns (firearms) should be eliminated from society. They are, of course, entitled to that position and, as such, unlikely to play or be involved with paintball.

Paintball markers are guns. There's just no way of getting around it. They use compressed gas to fire a (non-lethal) projectile. (Police and the military use specialized versions of paintball guns for training and crowd control. Even in these applications, the marker is considered non-lethal.)

Numerous other guns are used for fun: t-shirt guns, water guns, rubberband guns, BB guns, disk guns, dart guns, and more.

Anything that fires a projectile can be inherently dangerous if not treated properly. Fortunately, the paintball industry has accepted its responsibility and actively promotes safe handling practices through the use of safety equipment (goggles and barrel-blocking devices), as well as being actively engaged in promoting good, basic safety practices. When followed correctly, the equipment and procedures are a virtual guarantee of safety.

The paintball marker is not "bad" in and of itself; it can be put to improper usage, and it is possible to get hurt with one if not used properly, but the paintball marker itself can't be bad because the marker doesn't do anything. It's the people who do bad, or stupid, or irresponsible things.

Having permission to use a paintball marker can be an opportunity to learn respect for safety procedures, responsibility, and the difference between proper and improper use of a piece of equipment.

3. You don't need goggles when you play/Any kind of eye protection is Good Enough.

These are patently false ideas. Furthermore, anyone expressing these ideas has no experience with paintball, no respect for the safety of others, and no business being around you or your child.

Protective Eyewear is the only *mandatory* piece of paintball equipment required for use by every single commercial operation in the country.

The caliber of the typical paintball ("68" or .68 inches in diameter) is, unfortunately, just about the perfect size to fit inside an eye socket. This means that, unlike a baseball, golfball, racquetball or other sports balls, when you get hit in the eye, you actually get hit in the eyeball. Other sports balls may partially impact the eyeball, but the vast majority impact the area of the facial bones that protect the eye socket. The balls are too large in diameter to fit in between your cheekbone and supra-orbital ridge.

The damage done to an eyeball as the result of a direct paintball impact can be, and most often is, total destruction of the eye. (Cosmetic repair may allow the player to retain the eyeball and look normal, but that eye isn't seeing anything anymore.)

Using any eye protection not designed specifically for paintball use is irresponsible, dangerous and *stupid*. Beyond not being able to withstand the impact of a paintball, other goggles—shop goggles, shooting glasses, motorcycle helmets, ski masks, diving masks, military tanker goggles (and I've seen players trying to use them all)—will most likely shatter upon impact. Small pieces of plastic lens material will be carried into the eye along with the paintball and, being plastic, they won't show up under X-ray. This means that the unlucky victim has to undergo a session of having their eyeball probed while an ophthalmologist searches around for the pieces.

You might think that you'll be saving a few dollars. You might think that because your child will only be shooting at targets you can avoid this necessity. You might think that because you aren't actually playing, you can skip the mask. *Don't make this mistake, as the consequences will last for a lifetime.*

4. You don't have to check a marker's velocity: I already had it tested last week/I can guess the velocity by the sound it makes/my marker never changes its velocity/I want to shoot really far.

Paintball velocities are a critical component of maintaining a safe play environment. The faster a paintball exits the barrel, the more potential harm it can do.

Years ago, an organization called the International Paintball Players Association evaluated the force of the impact that a paintball had at different velocities (Before we knew any better, paintball velocities were unregulated and not monitored.). They determined that a maximum of 300 feet per second (or a little bit more than 200 MPH) kept the force of impact—even at extremely close ranges—within safe limits (presuming that the paintball itself meets the A.S.T.M. recommended weight standard).

Testing is done with a device known as a *chronograph*. The chronograph is capable of sensing a paintball as it leaves the barrel of a marker and determining its velocity. Invest in one and make velocity testing a regular part of your child's paintball play.

It is true that back in the early days, players used the sound their guns made or the sound the impact a ball made against a target, to test their velocity, but that was literally before the introduction of the chronograph. Today, handheld devices can be obtained for well under $100.

Beyond the obvious safety considerations, a paintball gun's velocity is critical to achieving optimum performance and accuracy. Anyone who objects to using a chronograph before a day of play either enjoys hurting people, doesn't care about their marksmanship, or is clueless when it comes to maintaining safety.

5. I need to freeze my paintballs so they'll be fresh for playing.

Patently false! The only reason to freeze a paintball before using it is to inflict pain. A frozen paintball will not shatter, and therefore it imparts all of its energy to the target it hits, unlike a ball stored at normal temperature.

Freezing paintballs seems to be one of those "cool" things that runs around the Internet every couple of years, and the industry has to endure numerous complaints from players who have been victimized. If you should happen to find paintballs in your freezer, throw them out. A frozen ball that's allowed to defrost will not be good for much of anything, least of all good for shooting out of a paintball marker

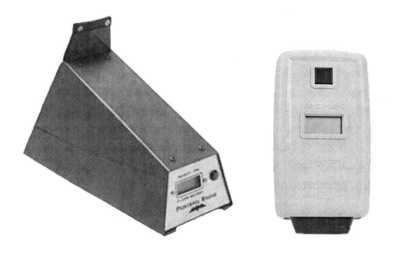

Figure 6. Paintball Chronographs. Both use Doppler radar technology to measure a paintball's velocity. The left hand image is a field chronograph and is built to be sturdy and last through tens of thousands of uses. The image on the right is of a hand held chronograph that retails for under $100 and is intended for personal and home use. Chronographs from Radarchron.

6. Plastic guns/Wal-Mart guns/paintball guns that sell for less than $500 are unfit for use.

Unfit for use is probably not the phrase your child used to state their opinion, but I'm sure you catch my drift... Cheap, easily broken paintball markers sold at large retailers have earned the derogatory nickname of "Wal-Mart Guns." While it is true that the large retailers (Wal-Mart, Galyans, Sports Authority, Target) stock inexpensive markers and other equipment, they have also begun selling an increasingly large number of quality products. A marker purchased at Wal-Mart is not necessarily a cheap gun, nor are certain brand names within the industry synonymous with making cheap product. Several companies do have extensive low-end product lines, but those same companies also offer quality product lines.

The Price Tag has become one of the cultural sign posts of modern paintball. "The more expensive something is, the better it must be." Or so many would have you believe. While this is true to some extent, it is also true that you can purchase good quality paintball gear for a reasonable amount of money, and you can find good gear at the larger retailers as well as at the specialty paintball shops.

7. Mass merchandisers are cheaper.

Not necessarily true. Some product sold by larger retail chains appears to cost less than most specialty paintball pro shops. I say *appears* because appearance can be deceiving.

For example, a large retailer may be offering a brand name paintball marker for, say, fifteen dollars less than the same brand name at the specialty shop. In reality, the two markers with the same name from the same company are not identical. The retail version has a few less expensive components, or is a stripped down version of the specialty shop model.

For someone not educated in the names and brands and features and qualities and accessories and mods and... one Brand X marker is not the same as another Brand X marker—reason enough to find and frequent a good specialty shop. Once you've acquired an education in paintball products, you'll be a better judge of what truly is less expensive at the retail chains.

8. Ordering on-line is cheaper.

Kids have a natural affinity for the Internet. It's been a part of their lives from the very beginning (not true for all parents), and is a major part of the immediate gratification culture that they live in. Purchasing gear off the Internet is one step away from wishing for something and having it appear in your hands.

It is true that there are many fine, honorable, and professional Internet retail sites; many of them appear to be selling for less than the retail chains and specialty shops.

Some web'tailers have established good reputations for themselves—while others are truly scams, with the rest running the gamut between. I'll cop out here and state the old saw that "If the deal looks too good to be true, it probably is." and ask you to keep it in mind.

On balance though, I've found that most players (and parents) would prefer to deal with someone in the flesh—someone who, in worst-case scenarios, they can hold responsible. The price difference between Internet savings and brick-and-mortar stores is growing slimmer as time goes by, and a knowledgeable player/salesperson can more often than not save you those few dollars by providing good advice.

Also, please beware of EBay and Internet sales scams. Play tickets are often offered that claim to provide discounts to fields across the country; check to make sure that the field you'll visit will accept the coupon before you buy it. Some offer links to wholesale sites for a fee; unless you have a wholesale account, you won't get a discount. Others offer pyramid scams (for $5, when your name rolls around you get a $500 marker...).

Use common sense. If you find a reliable on-line store— by all means, use them.

9. **People get *killed* playing That Game.**

Yes, there have been a few (three that I know of) well-publicized deaths associated with playing paintball. But every incident involved the improper use of paintball equipment.

Make use of and stress the importance of following the basic safety regulations associated with the game and its gear, make sure everyone else does the same, and be assured there will be no accidents.

10. Paintball glorifies killing/has a negative culture.

The psychologists, social workers and arbiters of morality will *always* find something wrong with anything unfamiliar to them. At one time, paintball was considered to be a fringe activity, yet another counter-cultural way for aging men to rediscover themselves. Today, it has grown from its fringe beginnings into a highly-respected, lucrative, and iconic member of the extreme sports world.

While some look at paintball and see a game involving guns and shooting other people, I look at it as the *most* civilized expression of our primitive selves. The need to hunt, aggress, dominate, survive, and secure our place by the fire has been harnessed and given full expression through a harmless game. It truly demonstrates that one of our most recent evolutionary developments—a thinking, critical and creative mind—has gained control over our basest, meanest, most primitive drives.

Paintball culture is an ever-changing and morphing one. In the beginning, when participants were mostly older, professional males, and the game was generally a test of manhood, the culture reflected its participants; male chauvinism, chest-thumping and a barroom mentality prevailed.

Today's paintball participants are mostly younger, between the ages of 12 and 24, more co-ed than ever, and often vibrant adolescents weaned on the electronic age. What they think is cool *is* cool, and there are just as many paintball cultures as there are other youth cultures. These range from the Goth to WWJD and every crowd in between. Somehow, when they're all brought together at major events, they manage to get along, have a good time, and usually behave and comport themselves in an acceptable manner—at least as much as kids doing anything do.

Marker: BT TM-7
Loader: Empire Prophecy
Barrel: TM-7 Barrel
Tank: Pure Energy 48 cubic
inch 3000k Nitrogen System

Marker: BT Delta Elite
Loader: BT Rip Clip
Barrel: Apex Barrel
Tank: Pure Energy 47 cubic
inch 3000k Nitrogen System

Marker: Invert Mini
Loader: Invert Reloader II
Barrel: Invert Nightstick
Tank: Pure Energy 70 cubic
inch 4500k Nitrogen System

CHAPTER 2:
PAINTBALL EQUIPMENT

THE BASICS

The equipment needed to play paintball is relatively straightforward when it comes to gear. You'll need a mask, a marker, a Barrel Blocking Device (BBD), an air tank, a loader (or magazine), and some paintballs.

We'll go through each one of these pieces of basic gear so you can understand what they're used for and how they work, thus enabling you to help your child make good purchasing decisions.

THE MASK

Hear this loud and clear: *the only indispensable piece of paintball gear* (besides the BBD) *is a paintball-approved protective mask.*

Believe it or not, you can play without a marker, without paint, without a tank, without a loader—but you can't play without a mask. (I frequently made players compete without their markers during practice and drills—they think I'm crazy, but they thank me later...)

Masks made for paintball are entirely different from ski masks, motocross masks, shooting glasses, welding masks, diving masks, gas masks, tanker goggles and anything else that might have the appearance of offering eye protection but that won't get the job done.

You may have heard that you don't need a mask. You may have heard that shop goggles are more than enough protection. Don't buy it.

Each and every paintball goggle system released to

the market goes through an extensive (and costly) testing and certification process to insure that it meets the basic requirements of protecting the eyes.

This includes such things as impact tests (because paintballs travel at over 200 mph), multiple impact tests, shock tests, and tests to insure that paintball spray and shell can't get into the eye.

When it comes to a mask—spend the dollars and get a good one. (Comfort will help insure that the mask stays on.) Make doubly sure you check for the approved for paintball use or the PEC (Protective Eyewear Council) seal of approval before buying. Read ALL of the instructions that come with the mask.

Don't let your child play until you are sure that whenever they play they'll wear that mask. Rescind playing privileges if you ever catch them playing without one

Read the "Before You Play" checklist (in the Appendices) and make sure you go over the section on Barrel Blocking Devices (the other absolutely required piece of paintball gear).

A Note On Care of the Mask

Because it is amongst the least glamorous pieces of equipment, masks tend to get neglected by their owners. This is doubly shameful, since a worn, scratched and dirty mask lens is not safe and hinders the ability of a player to play effectively.

In order to clean a mask, you really don't need to do anything other than take it into the shower with you. Rinse it under the hot water and then let it hang to dry.

If a deeper cleaning is required, it is best to remove the lens from the mask frame. Paint shell often gets caught up inside the mask where it can't be washed off easily.

Figure 7. Paintball Masks. top row—Tippmann Voltage, Kee Action Sports Invert, V-Force Shield. bottom row—JT USA Proflex, Empire Events, JT USA Radar mask

The lens itself usually has two different materials (or surface coatings) on it. The outer portion of the lens is hard and scratch resistant, while the inner surface is soft and can be easily marred. Use warm water, perhaps a little soap, and dip the lens into it. You can wipe the outer surface dry, but it's best to "dab" the inner surface in order to avoid scratching it.

Under no circumstances should commercial glass cleaners be used to clean a lens; these contain chemicals that can break down the plastic of the lens, destroying their ability to protect.

When the lens is placed back into the mask frame, check the attachment points for strength and for signs of wear. Lenses can often be difficult to put in and take out—but take your time and make sure it's done right; the attachment points are what keep the lens in the mask when it gets hit, so

Empire E'Vent

GOGGLE SYSTEMS

Extreme Rage X-Ray

20/20
Invert 20/20

X RAY
Extreme Rage
X-Ray PROtector

avatar
Invert Avatar

Photo Courtesy of Empire Paintball, Extreme Rage Paintball, and Invert Paintball.

you definitely don't want the lens falling out under repeated impacts.

Finally, most manufacturers strongly recommend that any lens that has been impacted directly by a paintball be changed out for a new one. The old one did its job by taking that hit; now it's time for it to retire. Because lenses can be fairly pricey, it's best to check out the replacement cost before buying a mask.

If you want additional information regarding the testing procedures and requirements for paintball eye protection, you can obtain the standards from the ASTM.

(www.ASTM.org—Paintball Subcommittee)

The general rules regarding the use of masks in formal play (fields, events) include a requirement for the use of a *full mask* and *goggle* system, which protects the entire face, ears and partially protects the neck. We used to play with only goggles or with a half-mask covering just the nose and cheeks, but that's no longer allowed. There is also an industry-wide prohibition against physically altering your mask in any way from the manufacturer's original design. (You can still paint it if you want to.)

THE BARREL BLOCKING DEVICE (BBD)

The barrel-blocking device is also called a *plug* or a *condom*. (Don't let that word put you off, you can call it a bag, a sock, or a jimmy if condom bothers you.) The basic idea behind a BBD is to place some kind of device inside or in front of the barrel of a paintball marker so that, in the event of an accidental discharge, the paintball won't go anywhere.

Over the past several years the preferred version of this device has gone from the *barrel plug*—a device which is pressed inside the marker barrel (usually made of plastic and fitted with rubber o-rings to insure a tight fit) to *barrel condoms*—a

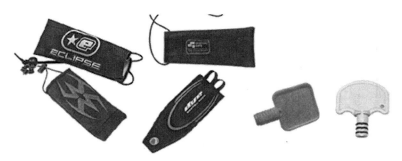

Figure 8. Barrel Blocking Devices (BBDs) Barrel socks from a variety of manufacturers—Planet Eclipse, Tippmann/SpecOps, Empire, Dye Precision and two styles of widely-issued generic barrel plugs.

bag made out of strong material and fitted with an elastic strap allowing it to be kept in place until removed.

Many marker manufacturers include a basic barrel plug in their packaging, while most commercial play sights and events require the use of a bag or sock. This disparity is a consequence of changes in insurance regulations covering the industry.

If your child just can't wait to shoot that marker, the barrel plug will do as a temporary substitute—but it's best to purchase a barrel condom as soon as you are able to.

The reasons for the change are many and include concerns that: a plug can be shot out of the gun with repeated firings; they are not that visible at a distance (making it difficult to determine if one is being used); they are often difficult to insert and remove (they need to be tight for a safe fit), making it likely that the lazy among us will not use them. Perhaps the most important difference is that you can't effectively display advertising on a barrel plug.

A good barrel plug will have 3 or more o-rings around it and will be difficult to push into the marker barrel unless the o-rings are lubricated a tiny bit. To insert one, twist it as you push it in. If that doesn't work, lick the o-rings a little (or lick a finger and then apply it to the o-rings).

Remove one using the same procedure—twisting as you pull it out. It's best to turn in a clockwise direction, as turning it in the opposite direction could unscrew the marker's barrel instead of the plug.

Putting on a barrel condom is even easier (and no, I won't go for the obvious joke here, although I'm sorely tempted…).

Find the *tensioning device* on the elastic bands and slide it as far away from the bag as you can (without removing it). Open the barrel bag and slide the barrel into it until it bottoms out.

Place the elastic bands over the marker so one is on either side of it and so that when the tensioner is slid towards the barrel; the elastic bands will hold the bag in place. To adjust the fit, pull the elastic bands towards the rear of the marker and, at the same time, slide the tensioner towards the gun.

Remove a bag by untensioning the elastic bands and then sliding it off of the barrel.

It is best to inspect your plug or bag on a regular basis. O-rings on the plugs can get worn and lose their friction, the bottom of the barrel bags can get frayed from repeated impacts, and the point where the elastic bands are sewn onto the bag can get frayed.

The barrel condom can be cleaned in the sink or in the washer (but don't mix it with anything other than paintball clothing…) and the plug can be washed out in the sink.

A Note About Safety

An excellent rule of thumb that has evolved over the years is: Before the masks come off—plug the marker.

Under any and all circumstances, it is **mandatory** that whenever paintball markers are in the presence of people who do not have masks, a BBD *must* be over each and every marker.

Paintball markers do not know who is wearing a mask and who isn't. It's also true more often than not that when the owner is convinced his paintball marker is unloaded and de-gassed—that's exactly when there's a ball in the chamber, ready to be fired.

The nice thing about paintball is that if you follow these two simple safety guidelines properly, there will be no permanent injuries.

PLUGS IN BEFORE MASKS OFF!

Just in case you weren't paying attention:

ANYONE WITHIN 300 FEET OF AN UNBLOCKED MARKER BARREL SHOULD BE WEARING A MASK

Some people seem to be of the mistaken belief that since they aren't playing in the game, they don't need to be wearing a mask. *Absolutely not true!*

If you are at a play site and are within 300 feet of the game, the markers and the players who are using them, it is mandatory that you are either safely behind a "ballistic barrier" (usually netting capable of stopping a ball) or are wearing a mask system. This holds true for indoor fields, outdoor fields, events, commercial sites, backyard sites and anywhere that you might be exposed to an unblocked paintball marker.

The length of exposure doesn't matter either; walking onto a netted field for even a second without a mask could cause loss of an eye. If you plan on attending playing sessions with your child—*even if you won't be playing*—it's probably a good idea to pick up an extra mask for yourself. If you use it properly, your child will be encouraged to do so as well.

A Note About Paintball Netting

Most fields have adopted "ballistic netting" as a way to

separate playing fields from non-playing areas; netting also has the added benefit of allowing people to watch games without having to wear a mask. But there are a few things to keep in mind.

Not all netting is suitable for stopping a paintball. You'd be surprised what a paintball can cut through— cardboard, ground cloth, tarpaulins, landscaping net, Plexiglas—even aluminum soda cans, which can be sliced in half by repeated paintball impacts. Netting used for paintball is specially manufactured for the purpose, and hung loosely to allow it to absorb the paintball impacts.

Netting degrades under direct sunlight. Field netting needs to be replaced every few years, as ultraviolet light breaks down the plastics used to make it. Old netting gets crumbly and will break or tear very easily. A field surrounded by old netting may look perfectly safe, but paintballs will cut right through it. If you are concerned, test a small section; inspect the netting for tears, holes, rips, etc. If you are suspicious of it, don't count on it to protect you.

Netting can have holes that will let paintballs through. More often than not, those holes or tears are located at places along the net that take repeated impacts. These are usually easy to spot, as the ground along the net will have a large accumulation of spent paintballs. Rips and tears also frequently occur at or near attachment points. Keep an eye on those locations and inspect the netting. *Don't stand right behind a spot along the net where it's obvious that a lot of paintballs hit.*

Don't lean against the netting when watching a game. Pushing your face right up against the net defeats the purpose of the net by not allowing it to move; you'll take the direct impact of any paintballs that hit the net where your face is pushing through.

Balls often bounce off of the inflatable bunkers used at

40

Figure 9. Paintball field netting around a competition field. This netting comes from the Alpha Netting company. Several other companies provide similar products.

most fields and ricochet off the field. These can often appear to have come through the netting (and usually have a pretty good velocity as well), but most likely bounced *over* it. Most fields have netting that is anywhere from 12 to 20 feet high (higher at some events), but the only real way to prevent all of the balls from leaving the field is to completely cover the field with netting, and in most cases that is cost prohibitive to the field owner.

If you study a field closely (especially during use), you'll soon be able to pick out the spots where you don't want to stand; they're generally in line with a large bunker close to your end of the field, that is taking fire from across the field. If the field is an active one, you can inspect the ground outside the field for accumulations of paintballs, and then stay away from those areas. (Don't park your car there either…)

THE MARKER

There used to be a day when players had a choice of only three paintball markers when it came to buying their own. Those days are long gone.

At last count, there were some 25 paintball marker manufacturers producing approximately 1.2 million paintball markers each and every year. Most of those markers come in multiple configurations and each of them probably has about a thousand aftermarket or upgrade options.

The person purchasing their first paintball marker faces a bewildering variety of options, features, accessories and price ranges. (Pricing is also confused by the ever-present battle between brick-and-mortar stores and the Internet.)

My first advice when purchasing a marker is—*don't*. Curb those urges to spend that money as fast as possible and do some research.

It's fairly common for a new player to purchase 6 or more markers during their first year of play while searching for the feel and features that meet their needs. This represents a lot of money, as most paintball markers lose 25 to 50% of their re-sale value once they are no longer new.

There's an easier and less expensive way to do your research and that is—go visit a commercial playing site.

Over the course of a weekend you'll have a chance to see tens, if not hundreds of different markers, each one customized with individual accessories, each one owned by a proud paintball player who will be more than happy to describe what they like, don't like, what they modified and what they are planning on doing to it next.

You'll gain an insider's appreciation of what features are important, the differences between different levels of marker and the kinds of accessories you'll most likely be purchasing soon.

Failing that, visit a local paintball store. Find one where the staff is willing to take the time to explain and demonstrate, and where they have a wide selection. Find out how long they've been playing, what they themselves use, and feel them out to determine if they are people whose opinions and advice you can trust.

My second piece of advice is this: if a birthday or holiday gift request is for a paintball marker—find out what make and model your darling child has in mind before you buy. If your child has been drooling over the $1000 markers in the magazines and you put a $150 marker under the tree, you'll go from hero to goat in the three seconds it takes the wrapping paper to come off.

By no means am I suggesting you purchase whatever your

child wants. What I am suggesting is that, since they have already done their research, you ought to do yours. If a top-end marker is beyond your budget or inappropriate for your child, save the gift for something else they want or need and instead, take them for a visit to the local paintball store (the one you researched before), and help them pick out something they and you will be happy with.

Types of Markers

There are basically four types of paintball markers. These are:

- Entry level (the Wal-Mart* marker)
- Mid-Level
- High-End
- Tournament Level

*Calling a paintball marker a Wal-Mart marker has become a term of derision over the years. It's no longer appropriate, since there are many fine markers sold through chain stores like Wal-Mart and Sports Authority, but it's hung on as an easy way to refer to "cheap, plastic marker."

Which is also misleading, as there are plenty of fine paintball markers that have plastic components.

You'll also have to contend with there now being two general classes of paintball marker—the *speedball/tournament* marker and the *scenario/mil-sim* marker.

This is a new and evolving development for the industry that has not quite sorted itself out yet. Perhaps the most confusing aspect of this is the fact that in most cases there is no real physical difference between the two—but there is a conceptual difference.

Paintball markers used for competitive play (speedball, team-on-team games, tournament play) are generally highly

Figure 10. Entry, Mid and High End paintball markers, Top row—Spyder Victor entry level marker, Tippmann Custom Model 98 entry-level marker, Smart Parts Ion mid-range marker. Bottom row—Spyder VS-1 mid-range marker, Invert Mini high-end marker, Planet Eclipse Ego high-end marker.

colorful and as small, light and tight as possible. (Tight refers to the overall dimensions of the marker; small and thin ones are desirable because they present a smaller target to opponents.) A tournament player expects to compete in an environment where speed and size are critical factors—and in an environment where coolness is a major thing.

Paintball markers used for scenario play (24-hour games, military re-enactment, role playing, big games) are generally larger, more military in appearance, and there are only two desirable colors—flat black and olive drab. This is because scenario players desire the ability to hide, are often involved in games where there is a military theme, and like to hang all kinds of accessories on their guns, such as sights, flashlights, night-vision gear, laser range finders, etc.

Most paintball guns will serve very well in either environment, and, in fact, most are designed to do so. But there are a few key factors to consider before purchasing a marker specifically for either type of play.

A good tournament-specific paintball marker will be capable of high rates of fire, will usually be an electronic marker, will have a very light trigger pull, and will have good industry support for customization and after-market accessories. It will be small and it will be light.

A good scenario-specific paintball marker will have a decent rate of fire, will often be non-electronic, will be robust, and will include options to add features such as sight rails, stocks and aftermarket accessories.

A good *in-between* paintball marker will be a marker that has after-market product support allowing it to be converted for either style of play.

Pump and Stock Class Markers

The original paintball markers were single-shot and hand-cocked and were essentially based on BB guns. Within a year of introduction, players were already modifying them to allow for increased rates of fire and increased magazine capacity through the addition of pumps (like a pump shotgun) and

Figure 11. Tournament/speedball and scenario/mil-sim markers. Top row tournament markers: Smart Parts Epiphany, Dangerous Power G3, Bob Long Technologies Marq, Alien Paintball Independence, DLX Technologies Luxe, Angel Sports Fly, Dye Precision DM9. Bottom row scenario markers: Smart Parts SP-1, PCS US-5, Tacamo AK-47, Scenario Dreams P90, Engler Custom Paintball Guns BAR, Tippmann/US Army Paintball Alpha Black, Tiberius Arms T-8.

gravity feeds (external devices that held a number of paintballs that were introduced into the breech under the force of gravity).

Pump action paintball markers continued to evolve until the advent of the semi-automatic marker that did not require two hands to operate. In recent years, many players have returned to pump play as a way to get back to the roots of the game and/or as a cost-saving measure (pump play generally involves lower rates of fire and thus a lower consumption of paintballs).

Stock Class play restricts paintball marker technology to its origins, foregoing the use of high-capacity air systems and bulk feed mechanisms.

Electronic Markers and Non-Electronic Markers

In 1990, the paintball marker entered the computer age with the near-simultaneous introduction of two "electronic" markers—the *Shocker* from Smart Parts and the *Angel* from WDP.

The key difference between these and other contemporary markers was the use of a solenoid operating a valve or a solenoid valve, with an integrated circuit controlling the action of the solenoid.

In non-paintball speak, what this means is that electronics and electronic components perform some of the internal actions of the marker, where those actions were previously all mechanical or pneumatic in nature.

Prior to the introduction of electronics, players were able to fire *as fast as they could pull the trigger*; a good player, with a highly-tuned marker, could achieve rates of fire as high as 17 balls per second (but not in a sustained fashion; what this really means is that *if* a player could keep pulling the trigger that fast for an entire second, they'd spit out as many as 17

Figure 12. Pump/Stock Class Markers: CCI Phantoms. Left—Stock Class. Note the 12-gram changer in front of the grip and the lack of a gravity feed. Right—Pump. Note the feed port for a gravity feed loader and the receiver for an air tank at the bottom of the grip.

paintballs. In reality, they achieved a rate of fire equivalent to 17 balls per second, but only for a brief portion of a second).

With electronics in the mix, players do not have to physically pull the trigger for each and every paintball they wish to fire. *Burst modes* were introduced (allowing 3 or more balls to be fired for each trigger pull), followed by what are now known as *firing modes*—of which there are hundreds, if not thousands.

A *mode* is a set of programming instructions, loaded onto a chip inside the paintball marker that takes over the firing of the marker from the player, once the player begins pulling the trigger.

Different leagues allow different types of modes—some limiting electronic markers to "one ball per trigger pull," while others allow *ramping* or *bouncing*.

Ramping is a mode that increases the rate of fire after specific sets of circumstances have been met. For example, after the player has pulled the trigger three times within a two-second period, the marker will fire at a sustained rate of 15.4 balls per second, so long as the trigger is pulled at least once per second. In other words, as long as the trigger is pulled once per second, the marker will spit out 15.4 balls during that second of play.

Bouncing (better known to players as trigger bounce) is an artifact of the electronic components used in the markers. Without entering into all of the debate and technical jargon that surrounds this issue (which served as the basis for the first arguments involving the introduction of electronic markers), it essentially boils down to this: when the electronic switches used in the markers are closed, they generate multiple signals, each of which can be read as an individual pull of the trigger. While the user may seem to only be pulling the trigger once, the electronic circuitry "sees" several pulls of the trigger.

Under the *one ball per trigger pull* rules, programming that eliminated trigger bounce was required in order to make the marker legal for use. Where that rule is not in effect, it is possible to use trigger bounce to increase a player's rate of fire.

By incorporating bounce, ramp and other programming features, electronic markers can provide a player with a highly controlled, highly accurate paintball marker with an almost unlimited rate of fire. Competition players who are always seeking an edge over their competition prize these qualities.

One major consequence of the introduction of the electronic marker is, of course, the increased consumption of paintballs. Generally speaking, a marker that can fire faster is going to be used in the fastest of all possible modes, which means that the player is going to need to purchase more paintballs for a day of play.

So far as buying decisions are concerned, the choice between an electronic marker and a non-electronic marker is not a simple one. The following needs to be taken into consideration:

(Generally speaking)
- A non-electronic marker is more user serviceable

than an electronic marker.
- A non-electronic marker is more easily maintained by the user than an electronic marker.
- A non-electronic marker is less expensive than an electronic marker.
- A non-electronic marker is less expensive to operate than an electronic marker.

On the other hand, electronic markers are all the rage, it is very difficult to compete effectively when you are out-gunned, prices for really good electronic markers are steadily declining, and most (not all) non-electronic markers are generally geared towards entry-level players. (Not to mention that electronic markers retain a higher re-sale value than non-electronics.)

The buying decision is, of course, yours; perhaps the most important consideration in making a choice is your assessment of how long your child is likely to be playing.

A Note about "Cheater" Boards

Over the past several years, numerous companies have introduced aftermarket circuit boards and/or programming for the various models of electronic markers. These are generally referred to as *cheater boards* because the first ones to come onto the market incorporated secret modes that allowed players to circumvent the rate-of-fire rules.

Of late, various leagues have banned some of these boards; additionally, competition leagues have introduced various technologies to catch players using illegal modes.

Some of the programming in these boards is very refined and they do introduce better ways (more efficient) to operate the markers. However, careful research is required before purchasing such an upgrade, with particular attention needing to be paid to whether or not the programming on such boards is considered legal by the various governing bodies of the sport. If the field that your child will play at most frequently disallows the use of cheater boards, it would be a waste of dollars to purchase one.

Electronic Markers and Non-Electronic Markers

There are only a few pieces of advice I can offer to help you make the decision on what kind of marker to purchase. Unfortunately, none of this advice is hard and fast, all of it is subjective and, despite the fact that I'd like to take this burden off your hands, I can't: the final decision is all yours.

Things to keep in mind when making this decision are:

* How interested and committed your child seems to be (tempered by what you know about your child's level of sticking to a new activity),
* How old they are,
* Whether they have played already or are just starting out,
* What kind of play they are interested in,
* What the group they are involved with is using.

Entry level markers range from approximately $50 to just under $100. Most of these markers are primarily of plastic manufacture, have few add-on accessories, and are for those who want to check out the game for a small investment.

Mid-Range markers run from just over $100 to just under $300; most are supported by numerous upgrades and accessories, and there are a number of both electronic and non-electronic models to choose from. Some models in this range are even considered suitable for competition play (although the versions used in competition are usually highly customized). A good mid-range marker can last a player for years, is well supported by the industry and generally commonly available. These kinds of markers are for the person who will play regularly, wants to have good equipment, but is not overly concerned about having the most expensive, best-of-the-best marker.

High-End markers start at just over $500 and go up from there. Some are souped-up versions of mid-range markers; others are specifically geared to the competition player. Most (if not all) are electronic. Unless you have an unlimited budget for recreational equipment, it's best to do a lot of research before making a purchase of this type.

General Rules Concerning the Purchase of a Marker

Most manufacturers now offer a 1-year warranty against defects in manufacture; however, it's best to check into the repair/replacement history of the company manufacturing the product. Like any other industry, consumer support ranges from terrible to outstanding. The more you have invested in a paintball marker, the more important it is to find out what kind of support it has in the industry—both from the manufacturer and from stores that sell them. (Do they stock replacement parts, can they do warranty repairs, etc.?)

Price has *nothing* to do with capability. The paintball industry operates in somewhat of a faddish manner: today, company A and everything they make, is really cool and every kid wants to wear that company's logo; tomorrow, company A will be dead as a doornail and company B is all the rage. I'd provide a list of all of the 'hot' companies here, but it would probably be obsolete by the time this book was printed. Keep in mind that the price of a company's products often has more to do with their advertising budget than with any relation to quality, features or capability. On the other hand, a company that has made a good name for itself is not doing so on advertising alone (*street cred* is important in paintball, and paintball's grapevine rivals the Internet for speed).

Although I hate saying it—what your child's friends and playmates have is almost as important as any other consideration. It's not just a question of keeping up with the Joneses or giving in to peer pressure. If all of the players your child plays with have high-end markers, your child will need one to be able to play effectively and competitively.

The marker a player has is often used by other players to determine how good they are (even though this is not a true indicator of skill or experience). If your child has ambitions of playing competitively, they will not be able to try-out for a team without a marker considered acceptable by that team. When picking sides the players with the least glamorous markers will be chosen last, etc. Perhaps most important of all: players who have inferior markers will often quickly lose interest in playing.

Most markers have a shelf life of a single season. The marker portion of the paintball industry is literally an arms race. In the beginning, it was possible to purchase a marker capable of keeping up with technological advances for two, three, even five years of play. Now, companies often introduce significant upgrades and model improvements on an annual (if not bi-annual) cycle. Careful attention should be paid to the stability and longevity of the manufacturer. Are new upgrades transportable to older models? Do they maintain a parts inventory for older models? How significant are the changes they introduce year to year? In general, the longer a company has been in the business making markers, the more user-friendly their product is from generation to generation.

Generally speaking, it's best to skip right over the entry-level markers if you believe that your child will be playing for any considerable length of time, be it one season or multiple years. (Keep in mind that the average teen's involvement with paintball is between six and nine months.)

Most mid-range markers have an upgrade path that will allow the user to add capability over time and will allow them to use the same marker for a considerable period. (Remember though that upgrading an existing marker is generally more expensive that purchasing the top-of-the-line model all at once.)

Most high-end markers will be good for a season or two, will retain a good portion of value on re-sale (depending upon vintage) and are a virtual necessity for the serious-minded player.

THE LOADER

The *loader* is a paintball marker's magazine. Fortunately for the beleaguered parent, there are only three types of loader. These are the *gravity feed*, the *agitating*, and the *force feed*.

In the early days of paintball, the marker's magazine was a tube arranged so that the paintballs would sequentially feed into the marker under the force of gravity. In the late 80's, various companies began to replace the tube with a *hopper* (some of the first loaders were made out of plastic quart-sized oil cans), again using gravity to get the paintballs to roll into the marker. One of the more successful designs introduced helped eliminate ball jam (several balls locking up with each other at the outlet point, preventing any balls from feeding into the marker) through the use of a very gently curved housing.

Ball jam was not really a major issue for many years, since the action of cocking and firing the marker (pump action markers during this era) tended to jostle the contents of the loader enough to insure a steady stream of paintballs into the breech. Rates of fire were slow as well (5 to 8 rounds per second), meaning that only a few balls had to be readily available in order to keep up with the player's firing demands.

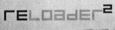

Today's semi-auto markers (electronic or otherwise) are very steady and have virtually no recoil action from firing. This means that gravity feed loaders have difficulty in keeping up with firing demands unless they are frequently shaken by the player between firing events.

While many entry and mid-level markers are initially supplied with a gravity feed loader, it's a pretty foregone conclusion that most players will want to quickly obtain an agitator or a force-feeder.

Agitating loaders were an intermediate step between gravity feed and force feed loaders. Essentially, these loaders used some type of mechanical mechanism to jostle or agitate the balls inside the housing; rather than the player having to shake the loader, the loader did its own shaking. Once rates of fire increased beyond the 18-20 balls per second range, not even agitators could keep up with the firing demands and it was necessary to create force feed loading systems which use motors and ball guide paths to force paintballs into the breech of the marker. Agitating systems remain on the market as inexpensive alternatives.

Figure 13. Loaders progressing from gravity feed to force-feed. Left—original 90 round ViewLoader gravity fed loader. 2nd from left—generic 200 round gravity feed loader. 3rd from left— VL-2000 agitating loader. Right—force-feed loaders. Top left— Dye Precision Rotor. Bottom left—JT Vlocity. Top right—Halo. Bottom right—Empire Prophecy.

High end markers are useless without a force-feeder, as their rates of fire are so high that a gravity loader or agitating loader cannot keep up. A high rate of fire coupled with poor or slow ball feed is a guarantee that balls will get chopped in half as they are loading into the breech.

Most every company that manufactures a force feed loader also makes a gravity feed loader. Gravity feed loaders are inexpensive (usually five dollars or less) and more often than not packaged with entry level and mid-range guns. Most entry level markers will not be negatively affected by the use of a gravity feeder. Most mid-range markers can get by with a gravity feeder but will be greatly improved by an agitating or force-feeding loader. *Again, a force-feeder is a necessity for a high-end marker.*

Agitating loaders range between twenty and fifty dollars. Force-feeders generally range in price from about sixty dollars to one hundred and sixty dollars. There are several models to choose from, with the key feature being the method of activation for the feed mechanism. Some use sound/vibration caused by the firing of the marker to activate, others utilize a set of electronic eyes to determine if a ball needs to be fed into the marker. Some high end markers do not produce a sufficient enough kick to activate the sound-based loaders, so it's a good idea to check with a storeowner or marker manufacturer before obtaining this accessory for a marker.

THE TANK

Once again, things were simpler in the old days (kind of like a marriage, pre-children). There was one source of pressurized gas, the same as is used in BB guns—the 12-gram CO_2 cartridge.

This is a disposable, aluminum cylinder containing 12 grams of carbon dioxide under 1800 pounds of pressure (1800

AIR SYSTEMS

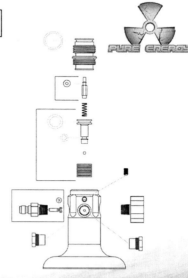

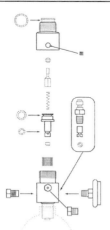

Co2 Regulator Schematic

Reactor III Schematic

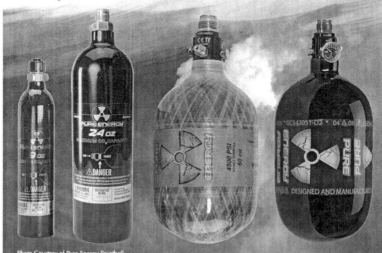

Photo Courtesy of Pure Energy Paintball.

psi).

Once loaded into the pressure chamber of a marker, these cartridges would be pierced, allowing the contents to flow into the valve chamber of the marker. Players could get anywhere from 15 to 50 good shots on a single cartridge, and, considering that the magazines used at the time rarely held more than twenty paintballs, this system was more than adequate for play.

However, several players were frustrated by the need to constantly change cartridges (not to mention the litter of expended 12-grams), and it wasn't long before the introduction of *Constant Air* (now generally referred to as *CA*, as in CA Adapter).

Constant Air is the use of a larger pressure vessel coupled to a valve system that can be hooked up to the valve chamber of a paintball marker. These pressure vessels range in size from 3.5 ounces to 40 ounces of gas (anywhere from 98 grams or more than 8 times the capacity of the 12 gram to 1120 grams or nearly 100 times the capacity of the 12 gram), with the most common sizes being 9, 12, 16 and 20 ounce tanks.

Carbon Dioxide remained the fuel of choice for paintball markers for nearly a decade and remains an inexpensive standby today.

Most players (and most markers) start out using CO_2, and this gas works quite well for the purposes paintball players put it to.

In the early 90's, a new power source—*High Pressure Air*—was introduced. Initially perceived as being "more dangerous" than CO_2, High Pressure Air (HPA) is now considered to be the better alternative for a wide variety of reasons.

A Note on Pressurized Gasses

None of the gasses used in paintball are toxic or flammable. Carbon dioxide makes up a good percentage of the Earth's atmosphere—animals exhale CO_2, plants inhale CO_2.

Carbon Dioxide is referred to as a *constant volume* gas; this means that under pressure, CO_2 will attempt to retain the same pressure across the volume it fills by turning from liquid to gas or vice versa. So, the interior pressure of a cylinder holding CO_2 will remain the same until virtually all of the contents have been exhausted.

A CO_2 tank filled to capacity is approximately 1/3 liquid CO_2 and 2/3 gaseous CO_2; CO_2 is commonly used in fire extinguishers and in making carbonated drinks.

High Pressure Air is the same air you breathe daily, under higher pressure.

Nitrogen alone has virtually the same properties as high pressure air (nitrogen makes up more than 80% of the Earth's atmosphere and is in every breath you take) and is frequently substituted for HPA.

HPA is used to fill SCUBA tanks at dive centers, and is not a constant volume gas; as gas is used, the pressure inside the tank declines. There is *no* liquid air inside an HPA tank, only gas under pressure.

All pressure tanks are rated and controlled by the US Department of Transportation. They must have a manufacturing date, a DOT stamp and certain functional features, including a valve and a *burst disc*, which is a safety device that allows the tank to safely vent if it is over-pressurized.

All pressure cylinders are manufactured under the supervision of the US Department of Transportation. If you are masochistic, obtain a copy of the *Code of Federal Regulations, Part 49*, so you can read all about the rules, regulations, certifications, restrictions and testing required in order to make one of these cylinders.

Where the rubber hits the road for the everyday paintballer is in obtaining fills (the act of putting gas into the cylinder). All of the bottles are supposed to be subjected to an inspection process prior to being filled by a trained technician. This process involves checking for unacceptable wear (dents that are too deep, scratches that are too deep and long, burn marks), the proper installation of the valve on the tank (it should not be separable from the tank using your hands alone), and the *Hydro Dating* must be within date—meaning that the tank must not be overdue for a Hydrostatic test.

A Note on Bottle Accidents

Chances are, you have heard rumors of people being killed or severely injured by a tank used for paintball. To date, I am aware of three such incidents (one which resulted in severe injury, the other two in death). While it is true that three incidents remains an extremely *low* number when compared to the millions who have played and been exposed to tanks under pressure, these incidents were preventable and should never have happened.

In all cases, the accident involved an improperly installed valve—one that was able to separate from the tank when the tank was under pressure. Familiarity with tanks and the simple testing methods required are all that is necessary to keep things safe. Here's how to make sure that you never experience an accident with a tank:

Before the tank has been filled for the first time (and insuring that it is not under pressure by opening the valve), attempt to unscrew the valve from the tank with your hands— no tools. If the valve turns even a little, *don't use it* and return it to the place of purchase. Follow this up with a routine inspection and test prior to every use.

Hydrostatic testing is the procedure of putting a tank under pressure (test pressure, which is higher than operating pressure) and checking to see how much the bottle expands. (Pressure tanks, even though they are made of metal and/or advanced composite materials, are literally balloons which expand when under pressure and contract when the pressure is relieved. You can't see or feel it, but it happens nevertheless.) If the bottle expands within acceptable limits, the tank is good for use; if not, the testers drill a hole through it so that it can never be used again.

All pressure cylinders have a re-test cycle (even if it is *no more testing required*), and those testing cycles fall into several neat categories based upon the type of tank. Those are:

CO_2 tanks *under* two inches in diameter (generally, anything under 12 ounces in size) never need to be re-tested, so long as they do not have visible dents, overly deep scratches, or burn marks.

CO_2 tanks *over* two inches in diameter (generally, anything 12 ounces or over in capacity) must be re-tested once every five years.

HPA tanks that are all-steel or all-aluminum (generally, anything under 50 cubic inches in capacity) must be re-tested once every five years.

HPA tanks that are "fiber wrapped" (carbon-fiber, fiberglass—generally anything over 50 cubic inches in capacity) must be re-tested either once every three years or once every five years.

Fortunately for the concerned and involved parent, most tanks (the vast majority these days) are stamped or otherwise permanently marked with a manufacturing date, a manufacturer's identifying mark, and the exemption code under which the tank was manufactured. (Exemption codes are US DOT speak for the regulations covering a particular manufacturing process.)

Figure 14. Air Systems. Left—the original power source, 12-gram CO_2 disposable cartridges. Middle—two different sizes of generic CO_2 tanks—20 and 12 ounce capacities. Right—different sizes of HPA/Nitrogen tanks: Left—Guerrilla Air. Right—Pure Energy.

Most stampings on CO_2 tanks look something like the following:

12 OZ CO_2 1C-3ALM 124 M5343 05^08

This translates to: 12 ounce capacity tank for holding CO_2, made under the low-pressure aluminum cylinder exemption, manufactured by company M5343, manufactured in May of 2008.

These stampings will either appear on the sidewall of the cylinder an inch or so below the neck or on the flat bottom of the cylinder.

Most markings on HPA cylinders are printed on a card that is then over-wrapped and are prominently visible on the side of the cylinder. They'll look something like the following:

DOT-E 10915-4500

EJ 120307 (Company Name)

6^08

Which means—made under exemption 10915 for 4500 psi tanks, made by manufacturer X, manufactured in June of 2008.

A re-tested cylinder that is re-approved for use will be permanently marked with a new stamping (sometimes a glued-on tag) with the name of the testing facility and the date that the cylinder was tested.

Re-testing is handled by DOT regulated facilities and generally costs somewhere between $25 and $45 per cylinder, plus shipping costs. For this reason, the practice of testing CO_2 cylinders has generally fallen out of favor, since a new CO_2 cylinder usually costs the same or less than the cost of testing.

HPA tanks, on the other hand, usually cost $100 or more, and are therefore worth re-testing. Most paintball retail shops and fields know of a re-testing facility—some even provide re-testing services.

Because of the requirement for testing, it is very important to *check the dates* on a tank that is being considered for purchase. While it is true that the vast majority of tanks make it through their first test (and subsequent tests—I have one tank I've used for nearly 12 years that has been re-tested three times), you wouldn't want to have to send one for testing immediately after purchasing it. A five-year tank that expires in three or four years, provided that it is being discounted, can be a good purchase.

A Note on How to Read the Testing Date

You'd think reading and calculating dates would be relatively easy, but experience on the street says otherwise. A five-year tank with a manufacturing date of 06/08 is only good until 05/13—*not* 06/13. This is because the manufacturing date is considered to be *inclusive* of the month of manufacture. Whenever you are reading a tank's date, add the appropriate number of years (three or five) and then subtract one month.

Remember that testing takes some turnaround time also, so keep an eye on that date and send it out for testing a few months *before* it's really going to be needed.

A Note on Tank Fills

Interestingly enough, while there are regulations covering the manufacture and testing of tanks, there are none regarding the filling of tanks. There is an organization that sets standards (the Compressed Gas Association or CGA), and everyone references the proper training and certification of fill technicians, but there's no school, government office or anything else to put a stamp of approval on this potentially hazardous activity, with the exception of industry-operated certification facilities. (One such is the Paintball Training Institute in Tennessee—www.paintball-pti.com.)

Most fill technicians are certified through in-house training, supervised by someone else who learned and was certified in the same manner—a sort of apprenticeship arrangement.

Most of the folks certified in such a manner have a good grasp of what they're supposed to be doing, but it doesn't hurt to watch and make sure that they're doing things the right way. Here's what to expect from a fill technician doing things *the right way:*

For CO_2 fills –

- The bottle must be inspected.
- The re-test date must be inspected.
- The valve should be hand-tested.
- The bottle should be screwed into the fill apparatus and hung from or placed on a scale.
- The tank should be chilled (placed in a cooler/ refrigerator prior to filling or filled with a small amount of gas and then purged).
- The scale should be zeroed.
- The tank should be filled to the stated weight and not higher (12 ounces of gas for a 12 oz tank, 20 ounces of gas for a 20 oz tank).

For HPA fills –

- The bottle must be inspected.
- The re-test date must be inspected.
- The valve should be hand-tested.
- The tank should be connected to the fill apparatus and firmly held in place by the technician.
- The fill apparatus should have a pressure gage that shows the pressure in the tank being filled.
- The tank should be filled SLOWLY.
- The tank should never be filled beyond its rated capacity (either 3000 psi or 4500 psi).

If done strictly according to the recommended guidelines, HPA tanks should be filled while resting in a water bath;

HPA tanks heat up during filling and the water helps prevent overheating of the tank. Very few paintball fill facilities use a water bath, opting instead for a slow fill method. Either method (when done properly) will result in a bottle that feels warm to the touch, but not overly hot.

Here are a few other things to keep in mind:

CO_2 tanks cannot be *topped off;* in other words, they have to be emptied and filled from scratch. If you want to be economical and efficient, weigh each tank when it is empty and scratch the tare (weight of the bottle and valve only) onto the bottom of the cylinder. When you aren't sure how much gas is left, you can always weigh it; the difference between the actual weight and the tare weight is how many ounces of gas you have left.

It is a common practice to fill CO_2 tanks to one or two ounces *below* their stated capacity; this is not a rip-off but a good safety practice on the part of the store or field doing the filling that allows some additional room for gas expansion inside the tank. Short filling of one or two ounces is ok— short filling of more than that either means the fill station needs more gas or you are being charged for something you didn't get.

Some stores and fields overfill CO_2 tanks and justify it as giving you a bargain; chances are it's going to cost you, so don't buy it. What you'll be getting back is an unsafe tank.

If purged too rapidly, a CO_2 tank can end up with a chunk of CO_2 ice (dry ice) inside; if you then fill it again without allowing that ice to warm up into liquid and gas, you can over-fill the tank. You can warm a chilled tank by placing it under running tap water. You can also hear an ice chunk by shaking the tank—it will rattle around inside.

HPA tanks should be filled with the tank sitting in a water bath—the recommended procedure to keep them from heating up too much. (HPA tanks warm up when filled, while

66

CO_2 tanks chill when filled.) Most paintball filling operations dispense with this part of the procedure by doing a slow fill. In reality, they just dispense with the water tank and do fills. Insist on a slow fill if at all possible.

Many people with HPA tanks make two additional purchases—a scuba tank and a scuba fill adapter—a fill adapter that mates to the SCUBA tank and has a fill nipple for HPA tanks on it. Fills of SCUBA tanks at dive shops usually run between $3 and $5, and the smaller HPA tanks can be filled numerous times from one SCUBA tank. If you decide to go this route—*please*—obtain instruction on the proper filling procedures from a local field or store.

All pressure tanks have a pressure relief valve built into them, usually called a *burst disc*. This is a nut screwed into the side of the valve that is sealed off with a metal disc designed to fail in a controlled manner if the pressure in the tank exceeds safe limits. These are replaceable (but it should be done by trained individuals). The burst disc allows the gas in the tank to vent in a controlled manner. If this should happen while you are around, here's what to expect: there will be a loud *bang* followed by the hissing of gas venting. If it is a CO_2 tank, a large volume of what looks like smoke or steam will be visible around the tank and the tank will become covered in ice. These things happening are what is supposed to happen and are a clear indication that your tank was either filled beyond its rated pressure or the tank was allowed to over-heat.

Don't: leave tanks in a closed car in the sun, leave tanks sitting in direct sunlight, store them under heaters or radiators, warm them up over a heater or fire, or disassemble them.

Do: store them and transport them with some kind of padding or protection around them. Many companies offer tank covers and they're a good investment.

A Note on Tanks in the Post 9/11 Era

Because of the high-profile accidents involving tanks, a new standard for tank valves was established mandating that every valve should be made with a *fast purge* system incorporated into its design. There have been several patents issued for the different ways to accomplish this. Essentially, a gas passage is built into the valve to allow all gas under pressure to vent from the tank if the valve begins to unscrew from the bottle. This will eliminate the bottle-rocket effect of a separated valve, provided that all tanks in use have such valves in them. Unfortunately, many tanks using the older standard are still and will remain in circulation for some years to come, so it is best to maintain good safety practices whether the valve is an old or new model.

The Transportation Safety Administration (TSA) has also had a profound effect on paintball, particularly among tanks. Valves must now be removable for transport or shipping by air so that the inside can be inspected. The industry has responded and all new HPA tank/valve systems are being manufactured in this manner, but, again, numerous older systems are still out there that are perfectly good for use but don't meet this requirement.

THE BARREL

I can't tell you the number of times that I have heard a parent ask their paintball child, "What do you need a barrel for when you already have one on the gun?"

Despite the damage that it will do to your wallet, I must reluctantly agree with your child and state that, chances are, they *do* need an additional barrel.

It's true that barrels are really nothing more than an open tube, like a straw for shooting a spitball, but the length and inner diameter of that tube is critical in gaining optimal performance from a paintball marker.

Despite the fact that paintballs are all advertised and described as *sixty-eight caliber*, the diameter of the ball varies considerably—from a low of .64 to a high of .689 (or greater)—and the fit of a ball to the barrel can have a dramatic effect on accuracy.

Over the years a number of rules of thumb for ball-to-barrel fit have been devised. A good fit can be described as one that allows you to blow a ball through the barrel with your mouth, requiring some but not a lot of force.

Ball-sizers have also been introduced (a guide you can drop balls through to gage its diameter). These are an excellent compliment to the multi-piece, multi-insert barrel systems that appeared on the scene a few short years ago.

The reason you need to purchase an aftermarket barrel is historical; gun manufacturers used to make their own barrels, usually as one piece with the breech portion of the marker. Screw-in barrels were then introduced, followed by several custom-barrel manufacturers, which in turn caused the gun makers to decide that they could offer a lower-cost product by providing a simple, basic barrel, knowing that most players would prefer to purchase a custom one.

Complicating matters is the fact that virtually every gun manufacturer insists on having a proprietary barrel thread. Chances are, the barrel from the old paintball marker will not fit into the new paintball marker.

Today, most barrel manufacturers offer barrel *kits*, usually consisting of several back pieces threaded to attach to a particular marker, several front pieces of varying length, and inserts or chokes that adjust the inner diameter of the barrel for the diameter of the paint being shot.

A good barrel kit is the best way to go, since, with the exception of the back piece (threaded for a particular marker) the whole kit can be used on any marker. If your child changes guns during their career, they can purchase a new back end, instead of having to invest in a whole new barrel system.

A Note on Barrel Length

With the exception of extreme climate conditions, the most efficient barrel lengths for a marker are those between ten and fourteen inches overall. (Longer barrels *do not* make for better accuracy. Properly tuned markers and the correct inner diameter, plus shooting good quality paint, make for better accuracy.)

Some players prefer longer lengths (16 to 18 inches), but this is not for accuracy; it's so they can use the barrel to push an inflatable bunker out of the way and shoot from a well-protected position.

Using a too long or too short barrel will negatively affect gas efficiency (requiring more gas to fire each ball), which can have negative effects on range and accuracy.

A good thing to do before purchasing an aftermarket barrel or kit is to contact the marker's manufacturer and ask them what makes of barrel and length of barrel they recommend.

If your child will be using one particular brand of paint the vast majority of the time, you can also contact the paint manufacturer and ask them the recommended inner diameter for barrels when using that brand of paint.

A Note on "Trick" Barrels

Over the years, several *trick* barrels have been introduced, claiming to offer better range, better accuracy, etc. Barrels that put a back-spin on the ball are amongst the most prevalent. While those currently manufactured do deliver on their promise of greater range, players need to remember that greater range does you no good if the ball is traveling so slowly that it usually bounces off of its intended target instead of breaking. Without getting into the physics of the whole thing, these barrels are designed to cause the paintball being fired to spin rapidly backwards. This spin creates lift, allowing the ball to travel further. However, the energy for the spin must come from somewhere, and where it comes from is the ball's inherent energy. The ball will travel further, but it will take longer to get there and will have less impact upon arriving. Rather than spending good money, I'd prefer to see players get their range the old-fashioned way, by elevating their barrels.

A Note on Ports, Rifling and Silencers

Ports (small holes drilled down the length of the barrel) were originally developed as a way to provide external rifling; the theory was that the gas escaping caused the ball to spin and increased its stability, leading to greater accuracy. We now know that barrel ports do only one thing: quiet down the report when a marker is fired. (They also make the barrel look *cool*.) Most barrels today are ported, but there is no accuracy issue when choosing between a ported or non-ported barrel.

Internal rifling (both of the straight and spiral variety) has also been tried on numerous occasions. Once again, the jury has determined that none of these methods causes the ball to spin (like a bullet). Some (particularly straight rifling) do seem to have a positive impact on accuracy, but the whys and wherefores have not yet been worked out. There's no need to seek out or avoid an internally rifled barrel.

Silencers are generally considered illegal, particularly if they could be retrofitted to a real firearm. The BATF states that such devices are illegal under Federal Guidelines. Whether this is actual law or an overly broad interpretation by the BATF is still being debated by the paintball community. However, with the exception of some scenario games, the opportunity to effectively use a silencer is extremely limited.

Figure 15. Barrels and barrel kits. Left—Pro-Team Products/ Armson SSR. 2nd from left—Smart Parts All American. Middle—J&J Performance The Edge barrel kit. Right—Smart Parts Freak barrel kit showing barrel sleeve inserts.

OTHER NECESSARY EQUIPMENT

THE HARNESS

The *harness* is a form-fitting piece of load-bearing gear that allows players to carry additional re-loads for their guns. They come in two basic varieties—the *butt-pack* and the *vest*.

Butt packs are by far the more popular version, for several reasons, the most important of which is that a well-designed pack places all of the paint (and the containers holding the paint) behind the player's body. This helps prevent breaks, because players usually present a portion of the front of their bodies to anyone who may be shooting at them. Clothing and skin are softer than plastic, so this arrangement promotes opportunities for bouncers.

Vests are generally modeled after tactical vests worn by the military and police, and are more often seen being used by scenario players; the vest was once the most popular method for carrying additional paint, but fell out of favor during the early 90's. It's now making a comeback.

A third alternative is the *pouch*. This is the least expensive option, since it involves purchasing a simple cloth pouch with a Velcro closure that can accommodate one, two or three pods (reloaders). These are worn on a belt supplied by the player.

Butt packs come in a bewildering variety of colors and styles. Some are quite expensive, while others (even some popular models) are relatively inexpensive. The primary considerations when purchasing a pack are the fit (most are designed like lumbar support belts with adjustable Velcro fastenings), the number of pods the player can carry and the orientation of the pods.

Two orientations are used—horizontal and vertical. Personally, I recommend the vertical pod arrangement (the pods stand straight up and down against the player's back) because it is much easier to remove a pod without exposing body parts, even when in cramped positions. (The player pulls down on the pod behind their back, allowing them to keep their arm behind their body while doing so. With horizontal pods, the pod must be pulled out to one side of the body or the other, which could mean that an arm or elbow will be sticking out from behind the player's cover while doing so.)

The number of pods carried by a pack are usually listed as #.#, such as 3.2. This means that there are three full pouches (a cloth enclosure that fits the pod) each with a separate cover (a flap of material with Velcro that retains the pod until use) and 2 elastic loops for holding two additional pods, fitted in between the pouches. A 5.4 pouch would have 5 pouches and 4 elastic loops, and so on.

Be careful though, as a description of "6+1" for a pack doesn't mean "six pouches and one loop," but 6 pouches and one additional, oversized pouch for holding an extra air tank. The plus sign is what differentiates this arrangement from the

Figure 16. Top row—packs. Left—R7 USA. Middle—Redz Comfort. Left—Nxe pod and tank pack. Bottom vests. Left— SpecOps. Middle—Flurry Industries. Right—GenXGlobal

pouch and tube varieties.

+1 pouch systems (4+1, 5+1, 6+1) are sold primarily to players who believe they will need more gas during a game than is supplied by a single air tank. The chances of this occurring are slim to none—with the possible exception of those few players who are on the field for multiple hours during a scenario game. Tournament rules usually disallow extra tanks and, while a scenario game itself lasts for 24 hours, the player who manages to "live" for multiple hours on the field is usually doing very little shooting, and is, therefore, someone who doesn't need a lot of gas. (These packs were originally created to support players who used *remote systems* for their tanks—a long hose connecting the back-mounted tank to the paintball gun.) When you consider that most markers will get 1000 to 1200 shots off of a standard tank, a player would need to be carrying 8 or more pods of paint to exhaust one. These days, most folks who have these pouches just shove a couple of extra tubes into the +1 pouch; unless your child has a remote system, will **really** be shooting more than 1200 balls per game or just plain likes the pack, I'd recommend another design.

Packs usually are more expensive when they are of better quality—usually. The best product lines are made to withstand the rigors of play, be adjustable for the wearer, and are intelligently designed (all pods are hidden behind the body, extra support and padding for the spine is provided, extra stitching at wear points, etc.); inexpensive packs are generally cheaply made and reveal themselves with lack of adjustability and a poor arrangement of the pod pouches.

Vests are pretty much the same; each model will describe how many tube or pod pouches it has, as well as specialty pouches (for example, a pouch to store keys, wallet and barrel condom in), will have some padding and, again, good vests will be made of quality manufacture.

The number of pods that a player should carry is best

determined by their playing style; players who spend most of their time providing cover fire will need to carry more paint; aggressive players will need to carry less.

Pods hold an average of 140 paintballs, and most players will need an average of 500 rounds per game (not that they'll shoot it all, but for backup purposes as well). The loader holds about 200 rounds, which means the average player will need a pack or vest that can hold a minimum of 3 pods.

PODS

Pods used to come in all shapes and sizes—50 rounds, 75 rounds, 100 rounds, 140 rounds, flip-top lids, sprung lids, ergonomic shapes, padded, sound-deadened, and on and on. Today, they come in two sizes—100 rounds and 140 rounds—with the 100-rounders rapidly fading from the scene. Players and the industry have worked together to arrive at the "ultimate" refill size of 140 rounds, and all of the carrying gear has followed suit.

Pods are best purchased in large quantities, as the price drops dramatically when they are purchased in bulk. It's true that the average player can only use a few at a time, and they are re-usable, but most folks would rather spend a dollar or two on a small quantity than as much as ten dollars per tube when purchased retail.

On average, a regular player can expect to lose or break about 20% of their pods during the course of a day, so, again, purchasing in bulk is recommended.

Pods come in all kinds of colors, some with injection-molded logos, but they all work the same way, and unless your child is *really* trying to make a fashion statement, the color of the pod doesn't impact anything.

Figure 17, Pods. Left—Dye Precisions locking lid. Center— Smart Parts Transpod collapsible. Right—GenXGlobal generic 140 round pods.

A Note on Packs and Pods

If you are reluctant to invest in packs and pods for your child, there are a few tricks you can use to get by.

Cargo pocket pants (army pants) have cargo pockets that you can fit two or three pods into; it's not the greatest solution, since the pods become hard spots on the body which make it easier for paint to break on, but it is a temporary solution.

Football. Take two pods and tape them together (so the lids are opposite from each other), and then attach a short strap between the two; this arrangement can then be easily carried in the non-gun hand until used.

Stash. Carry a bag of paint onto the field and then stash it next to the flag station.

Restrict play to *hopper* ball. Players may only use the paint in their loader, with no reloads allowed.

PROTECTIVE PADDING

Most sports allow players to wear some level of padding for general protection, and paintball is no exception. Certain padding is a very good idea for safety-conscious parents, and padding has the added benefit of creating additional opportunities for *bouncers* (balls that hit but don't break).

Serious, seasoned players wear as much padding as is allowed under the rules specifically because of the bounce effect (and also because they're playing in a pretty harsh, aggressive environment).

The most commonly seen pads are: neck protector, knee/shin guards, forearm/elbow guards, beanies or other hats and gloves. The most commonly unseen padding is groin protection for males and breast protection for females. Chest protectors are available, but are not commonly worn by regular players and are viewed with disdain—the general concept being, if you need that much padding, you shouldn't be playing.

Neck protectors are strongly recommended—throat shots hurt. Most are neoprene with a Velcro closure and run under ten dollars. You can get by with a bandana wrapped around the throat, or even a scarf.

Knee/shin guards were originally introduced because of the large amount of crawling players did. Now they serve as an aid to sliding and diving. A good pair of volleyball kneepads are an acceptable substitute for the name brand pads (which usually run over $50). They're cheap and good for kneeling and crawling, but will not serve for sliding.

Forearm/elbow pads are also good for protection during the more aggressive styles of play; regular off-the-shelf pads will serve just fine.

A "beanie" (woolen hat) is a must; head shots are painful and players—especially the more aggressive ones—usually take a fair number of shots to the noggin during a day of play. Any wool hat will do.

Good gloves are important also (knuckle shots are among the most painful), and the newer gloves provide full hand/finger protection these days. Any gloves will do, but sports

Figure 18, Protective Padding. From left to right—BT neck protector, JT chest protector, Proto Paintball chest protector, Redz Comfort glove, Empire elbow pad, Invert knee pad.

gloves are the best.

Groin protection is a must for males. A hand towel draped over a belt like a loincloth is acceptable protection, but a soft-sided, martial-arts-style cup is strongly recommended (it provides front, side and bottom protection, unlike a regular athletic cup, and is more comfortable than a regular cup). As a parent, I'd insist on one; after all, you're protecting your future grandchildren...

Breast protection is important for females as well. In this case, the chest protector is probably a good idea. An alternative is a sports bra, under which a small folded towel is placed.

In general, you **do not** want to use "hard" forms of protection; roller-blading pads, gardening pads and similar styles of padding usually do not have the same freedom of movement built into them, do not stay in place during play and, rather than promoting bouncers, contribute to breaks.

Again, the type and amount of padding your child will require will be directly related to how aggressively they play. I'd suggest a neck protector, beanie and gloves (as well as sex specific padding) as a good place to start.

FOOT WEAR

Like every other piece of paintball equipment, foot wear

has evolved from the non-existent to the specialty product. Back in the early days, anything that seemed to fit the bill was worn—combat boots, construction boots, sneakers, track shoes, hunting gear.

The primary thing we were looking for in a shoe was an all-terrain capability—something that would serve well in the woods, in the swamps, in the streams, the snows of winter and the heat of summer...

The most popular solution was the combat boot, particularly those known as *jungle boots* or *snake boots*—foot wear that had been developed to deal with a tropical rain forest environment.

As time went by other considerations came to the fore. Ankle support was deemed to be mandatory: paintball players tend to put a lot of stress on their ankles. Weight became a factor as well since even a few less ounces on your feet can increase your running speed by a good couple of seconds.

Finally, in the early nineties (with the introduction of the concept fields), tournament players began adopting various types of athletic shoes with cleats for the gripping and running speed advantages they provided.

Today—any kind of foot wear will do for basic play. Some players have even been known to play barefooted or in sandals (or those toed "ninja" sox), although I don't really recommend those solutions.

The important things to look for are light-weight construction, durability, and good ankle support. Like the early days, combat boots are an ideal solution (especially considering that they can usually be picked up for an affordable price). For tournament players, 3/4 or full height soccer or softball cleats (these are the sports they are marketed to) are excellent solutions. Most leagues and fields ban steel or "hard" cleats, so look for the kind of shoes that have molded-in soft or rounded cleats.

GEAR BAGS

It should be pretty obvious by now that if your child has acquired even half of the equipment previously mentioned, they're going to need something to carry it all around in.

Over the past few years, the product manufacturers have introduced a bewildering variety of gear bags designed with the paintball player in mind. These range in size from *gun bags* (only hold one gun) to *monster* bags that will almost literally hold a ton of gear.

Most are either backpack or rolling-duffle style sports bags; custom paintball bags have specialized compartments built into them for protecting masks, markers, and tanks and other paintball specific features (such as pod pockets, padded paint compartments.)

They all also have one thing in common—a higher price tag than similar luggage because of the logo.

If your child has acquired enough gear to justify graduating from the pillowcase to a gear bag, check out rolling duffle sports bags (30+ inches in length being a good size), made out of cordura nylon. These will be more than adequate for your child's needs until they can earn enough yard work money to buy their own. (I got one of the aforementioned at Wal-Mart for $16 over five years ago and am still using my *ghetto* gear bag today...)

TOOLS

All players need tools. Most markers are held together with Allen-wrench-headed screws, and, if nothing else, they need a good set of Allen wrenches (both standard and metric).

A really good toolkit will have most, if not all of the following:
- Box wrench set (standard and metric)

- Small-sized screwdriver set (Phillips and standard)
- A clamping wrench of some kind (vise grip)
- Tools specific for their marker (usually included with the marker or available from the manufacturer)
- A roll each of duct tape, electrical tape and Teflon tape
- Marker parts (wear parts, such as seals)
- Lube (appropriate to the marker)
- Cleaning supplies (rags, paper towels)
- Squeegee or swab

My toolkit has hammers, a pipe wrench, a voltage meter, extra batteries (and chargers), a handheld chronograph, a huge box of unsorted screws, bolts, nuts, springs and various marker parts, an electric screwdriver, an electric drill, a soldering iron, a table top vise, a ratchet set and various bits of other things.

Your child won't need as much (I support a *team* with all of that gear); a basic set of tools, replacement parts, lube and tape ought to be sufficient for most needs.

PAINTBALLS

A rose is a rose is a rose. A paintball is *not* a paintball is not a paintball.

Paintballs are made out of gelatin, polyethylene glycol, sorbitol, starch, food coloring, vegetable and fish oils. They are made to be totally non-toxic and environmentally friendly.

For those who observe religious dietary laws (the Jewish *kashrut* (kosher) and its Islamic equivalent—*halal*), paintballs are **not** acceptable, as some of the gelatin is derived from horses and pigs—but then, you weren't going to eat them, were you?

Paintballs were originally filled with an oil-based paint, since they were intended for semi-permanent marking

PAINTBALL PERFORMANCE

Paintball Performance can ultimately be measured by examining the four elements that characterize paintball performance: Accurcy, Marking Ability, Consistency and Shell.

ACCURACY
- Specially formulated viscosities
- Ideal weight-to-ball ratio
- True trajectory from start to finish

MARKING ABILITY
- True color gamut for highest quality available
- Fills rated in wipeablility (hardest-- easiest to clean)
- Non-toxic and biodegradeable

CONSISTENCY
- Specially formulated outer core
- Prevents clumping
- Ensures dynamic appearance

ADVANTAGE SHELL
- Patented shell formula
- True ±.005 round .68 caliber paintballs
- Breaks on impact

Photo Courtesy of RPS-paintball.com

purposes. (Gelatin is hydrophilic, meaning that it likes to absorb water, and when it does, it swells. Using oil-based pigments therefore presented no problems.)

The RP Scherer Corporation, working with Pursuit Marketing Inc (PMI), introduced the water-based paintball at the end of the 1983 season—and this is one of the many technical innovations that have led directly to a wider acceptance of the game. (Very few people wanted to have to take a turpentine bath after a day of play and oil-based balls were heck on the wardrobe budget.)

At the present time, there are approximately six paintball manufacturing companies on the North American continent, and an equal number in Europe and Asia. There are perhaps three times as many private-label distributors of paintballs (folks who contract to have their own brand of paint packaged for them by one of the manufacturers).

As with almost everything else paintball, the brand name of the ball seems to be the number one factor in deciding which paint to purchase.

The best overall guide for purchasing paint is—spend the least amount of money you can for the performance desired. The next best suggestion is: pick a brand you like and stick with it.

Paintballs range in price from 1.5 to 6 cents per ball. Freshness is a key for optimum performance, so ask how long the paint has been in stock.

Don't be surprised if a facility you visit only allows players to use the paintballs that they sell. This is a common practice and one of the few ways a field owner has to make some profit.

Again—use your own judgment when shopping for paint, but remember that it's at least a couple of pennies out the barrel every time the trigger is pulled; the more accurate a paintball is, the fewer shots required.

A Note on the Buying, Care and Feeding of Paint

As mentioned earlier, most commercial paintball facilities require the use of paintballs that they supply. This is known as "field paint only," meaning you can not purchase paintballs elsewhere and use them at the field. No doubt you will find that fields charge more than other options (online, mass merchant store), but despite this, Field Paint Only is what you will find at most facilities. This is done for two good reasons: fields need to make a profit and selling paintballs is one of very few options open to them. The second reason is safety and liability. By instituting a field paint only policy, the field owner can control (more easily) what kind of projectiles their customers are shooting at each other.

The benefits to the player are admittedly secondary; if the paintballs at the field are bad, at least everyone is shooting the same bad paint; rental customers can be assured that the paintballs will shoot well from the markers they are renting and, at the end of the day, the field owner can stay in business and continue to offer a place to play.

Some fields do allow outside paint (Bring Your Own Paint or BYOP) while still others offer players the option of purchasing the field's paint or paying a small extra fee to bring in their own. (This is typically five to fifteen dollars, so add that to the cost of paint you purchase before determining if this is a good deal.)

Regardless of how the paint gets to the field, there are a few hard and fast rules for ensuring that they perform as well as can be expected.

First, paintballs have a shelf life and fairly strict storage requirements. The preferred environment is one that has about 50% humidity and a temperature between 55 and 65 degrees Fahrenheit. This should be a stable environment (not constantly fluctuating) and one that is out of direct sunlight.

Since very few people have a storage facility capable of providing these requirements, it is a good idea to only purchase as much paint as you will need for a day of play, or a weekend of play at most. (This can be calculated fairly easily by multiplying an average game's paintball usage by the average number of games played in a day. Beginners typically use between 150 and 300 paintballs per game, while tournament players may average closer to six hundred, seven hundred or even a thousand or more balls per game, depending on the position they play. Most commercial facilities want players to get their money's worth and will therefore encourage them to play as many games as possible—often ten or more—so assuming that even a beginner will need close to a full case of paint (2,000 paintballs) for a day's play is not unusual.)

Once paint has been purchased, a good temporary storage location should be found. Weather (temperature and humidity) can greatly affect a paintball's performance. Cold weather causes the gelatin to contract, making the ball smaller. Warm weather causes the ball to expand, making the ball larger. Relatively high humidity will give the gelatin an opportunity to absorb moisture from the air and will cause the ball to swell and get rubbery.

Most playing facilities do not have climate controlled storage space for customer paint so, especially if the weather is not cooperating, the player will have to bring one with them. The cheapest and easiest method is a medium-sized Styrofoam container—the kind used for picnics. The Styrofoam provides pretty good insulation and a pretty good moisture barrier. On very hot days, a coolpack/freezerpack can be placed inside the container to keep the paint cool. A small jar or some packets of dessicant can be placed in there as well to suck up excess moisture.

When using paintballs, it is best to keep them in their original container for as long as possible. Most paintballs are packaged in a carton that contains four five-hundred round bags of paintballs. Don't open all of the bags at the same time (unless you are going to use all of that paint right away). The plastic bags used for storing paintballs are not typical plastic—they are designed specifically for protecting paintballs from moisture. In other words, Ziploc baggies may be more convenient, but they don't do as good a job.

Be careful when transporting paint, loading it into the marker or putting it back into storage; the less handling the better. And get used to throwing away paint that has hit the ground. Sometimes you can brush it off, but most seasoned players would rather take the hit on paint than have to clean or repair their markers later.

WHAT TO PURCHASE, WHEN TO PURCHASE

The table following breaks paintball gear down into three categories—gear that you can't play without, gear that is good to have but that can be skimped on by a budget-conscious player, and gear that would be nice to find in your inventory, but won't stop you from playing if you don't have it. (By comparison, see the list of what a tournament player has in their gear bag.)

ABSOLUTELY NECESSARY	GOOD TO HAVE	NICE TO HAVE, BUT NOT (entirely) NECESSARY
goggles	goggles	goggles
barrel blocking device	barrel blocking device	barrel blocking device
marker	marker	marker
loader	loader	loader
tank	tank	tank
	ankle supporting footgear	cleated, ankle supporting footgear
	padded gloves	padded gloves
	neck protector	neck protector
	butt pack	butt pack
	pods	pods
	squeegee/swab	squeegee/swab
	marker-specific repair kit	marker-specific repair kit
		knee pads
		elbow pads
		'slider' shorts
		custom playing pants
		custom playing jersey
		complete toolkit
		scuba tank(s)
		scuba fill station
		paintball magazine
		extra goggle lenses
		'back-up' marker
		custom gear bag

A TOURNAMENT PLAYER'S GEAR

This applies to the scenario player as well; it's really a list of what the well-dressed paintballer with no budget limitations will be toting around.

Gear Bag	$80 - $150
Goggle bag (one per goggle set)	$35
Barrel bag	$45
Tool Kit (all tools needed to repair all equipment)	$50-$250
Spare parts kit (replacement parts for all components of markers)	???
2-3 top-of-the-line paintball markers	$2500-3500
2-3 HP air tank systems	$400-800
2 pairs of goggles	$150
2 replacement lenses	$50
multiple swabs	$25
1 pod swab	$20
2 pairs of playing pants	$225
3 team jerseys	$250
2 pairs of slide shorts	$100
1 pair of knee/shin guards	$75
1 pair of elbow-forearm guards	$50
2 neck protectors	$15
1 pair of cleated shoes	$90
2 battery chargers	$50
several packs of 9 volt and other batteries	$30
2 forcefeed loaders	$275
at least one barrel kit	$150
a couple of bandanas and/or a couple of beanies	$20

Or somewhere between $4500 and $7500 per player. (This kind of puts things in perspective when you're facing a request for a $150 dollar paintball marker, doesn't it?) Not to mention paintballs and airfills when at the field, the typical regular player will spend between $5 and $15 for all-day air fills and will purchase an average of a case-and-a-half (3,000 rounds) of paintballs, to the tune of somewhere between $35 and $80 for the day. $7500 in gear and $65 per day of practice—ten thousand dollars can easily be spent in a year.

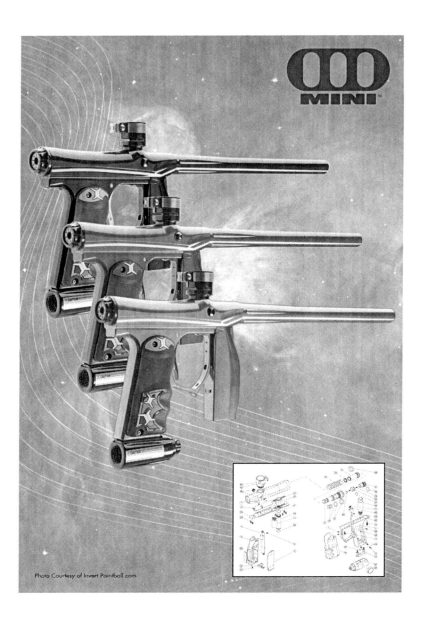

CHAPTER 3:
PAINTBALL TECHNOLOGY AND HOW THINGS WORK

This section is going to provide a *very* basic overview of the general concepts engineered into important pieces of paintball technology. It's not going to turn you into an overnight airsmith (also known as a gun tech—paintball terminology for marker and other technicians servicing paintball gear), but it will give you a little insight and hopefully keep you from making costly mistakes with equipment.

In general, I recommend doing the following when it comes to repairs and maintenance of paintball gear:

- Read the manual, read the manual, read the manual, visit the on-line support sites, read the manual, read the manual, consult with a local airsmith and then—read the manual.
- Prepare a well-lit, level work area.
- Supervise your child until they have shown mastery.
- Never, ever, ever work on loaded guns, filled tanks or systems that are under pressure.
- Never, ever, ever disassemble something until you are familiar with what you are doing (and then question the wisdom of doing so).
- Supervise—don't do it yourself. Let your child figure it out. After all, you don't want to become the family airsmith, do you?
- Follow the manual's instructions for disassembly; later you can figure out the shortcuts.
- Lay parts out on a towel so they won't roll; have cleaning supplies handy (paper towel, water, alcohol).
- Never force anything; if you can't remove a part using normal force with the recommended tools, you ARE doing something wrong.
- Consult with the local techs and read the manual.

I *strongly* recommend that players learn how to disassemble, clean, replace worn parts, and reassemble their own paintball markers. It can be a good time to learn lifelong skills (like reading the manual), instill a sense of ownership, and may reveal a budding engineer or designer in the family.

I recommend *against* home modifications of markers until the player has acquired a good technical knowledge of the principals and machinery involved. I've seen quite a few very dangerous horror shows built in the basement, with the proud inventors totally oblivious to how at risk they and everyone around them are.

There are many fine technical classes available for players who wish to take their paintball careers in a different direction. If your child is technically inclined, it might well be worth your while to investigate them.

HOW MARKERS WORK

All paintball markers operate on the same basic principles: a paintball is introduced into the breech and the action of the marker causes the paintball to be pushed into the barrel, while at nearly the same time a valve is opened, introducing pressurized gas into the barrel behind the paintball, which fires the ball. Action of the marker then returns the mechanisms to the pre-fire state, so that everything can start all over again.

In general, all paintball markers have the same components, regardless of whether they are pump-action, semi-auto or electronic in nature.

A *feed port* provides an opening into the breech of the marker. This is usually located at the rear of the barrel portion of the marker. Most feed ports are located on the top of the marker these days, although they can be located at various angles on the sides as well. (Some markers even have adjustable feed ports so that the user can adjust their location.) The feed port usually incorporates a *feed tube* as well, a cylinder projecting out from the marker. This is used for attaching a loading mechanism or magazine.

The *breech* is an area attached to the rear end of the barrel of the marker. Slightly larger than a paintball in size, the breech provides room for a paintball to drop into the marker from the loading mechanism. Most breeches are equipped with a ball detent, a small, flexible device that prevents the paintball from prematurely rolling into the barrel of the marker. (Ball detent is the common name, another being anti-doubler, so called because it prevents double feeding of paintballs into the barrel. Anti-doublers take many forms, from an actual ball bearing to fingers, wires, beads and other mechanisms. All work in the same way by filling up some of the space in the breech with a flexible mechanism.)

Behind the breech is a *bolt*. Usually cylindrical in shape, the bolt is arranged in the marker so that it can slide between an open position (allowing a ball to drop into the breech) and a closed position, which simultaneously seals the breech from the outside and pushes the paintball into the barrel. Usually, the bolt has a gas port located on one side (the bottom in most cases) for channeling pressurized gas from the valve through the bolt and out its face or front end (the portion of the bolt that pushes the ball into the barrel).

Attached to the bolt (more often than not by a removable pin) is the *hammer* or *striker*. When cocked and ready to fire, the hammer is usually under spring tension and locked into place. When the trigger is pulled, the hammer is released. Under action of the spring, the hammer strikes a valve, causing the valve to open and fire a paintball. Excess gas (*blowback*) then pushes the hammer back against the spring, re-cocking the marker for the next shot.

The trigger almost always acts directly upon a *sear*—a spring-actuated lever that holds the hammer in place against its spring tension. When the trigger is pulled, lever action causes the sear to release the hammer.

The valve is usually contained within a separate housing within the marker, and generally consists of a *valve body*, a *valve pin*, a *valve seal* (also known as a *cup seal*) and a spring. In operation, the cup seal is mounted on one end of the valve pin. The valve pin passes through the valve body and a portion of it extends out beyond the face of the valve. The valve spring holds the cup seal up against the body of the valve, creating a seal and preventing it from leaking. The action of the hammer striking the valve pin pushes the pin back against its spring, allowing some gas to vent through the valve. Immediately following the opening of the valve, the valve spring pushes the cup seal back against the valve, stopping the flow of gas.

In actual practice, the actions described above take place in the following manner:

- The user pulls the trigger rearward.
- The sear is depressed through trigger action, releasing the hammer.
- The hammer, under spring tension, begins to move towards the valve.
- The bolt, connected to the hammer with a pin, moves forward, pushing a ball from the breech into the barrel.
- The hammer strikes the face of the valve (with the bolt now sealing the barrel).
- The valve pin is pushed back from the valve.
- Pressurized gas flows around the valve pin, through the valve, up through the bolt and out the face of the bolt, firing the paintball.
- Spring action closes the valve.
- Blowback gas pushes the hammer back against its spring, pulling the bolt with it.
- The sear locks back up on the hammer, preventing

further travel.

- The breech is cleared by the bolt, allowing another paintball to be loaded.

There are, of course, numerous variations and different methods for operating a paintball marker, but all of the previously described mechanisms are present in one form or another. In electronic markers, the trigger may not be directly acting upon the sear—an electronic switch might activate a solenoid that trips the sear. In other markers, gas may be used instead of the various springs mentioned, or other pneumatic components (three-way valves, pneumatic rams, spool valves, pilot valves, regulators, etc) may replace some or all of the mechanical operations.

HOW ELECTRONIC MARKERS WORK

The mechanics of most electronic markers are the same as non-electronic markers, with the mechanical sear/valve mechanisms replaced with a micro switch and a solenoid or solenoid valve. These are electronic devices that function much like electro-magnets; when power is introduced to a coil, it becomes energized and creates a magnetic field. This magnetic field is used to open or close a valve and/or trip a sear. The complicated portions of electronic markers are the circuit board and associated programming. Basically, there's a mini computer sitting inside the grip of each electronic marker. Like a computer, the integrated circuits can be programmed to do just about anything you can imagine (iPods integrated into paintball markers are probably not all that far off in our future…)

The latest craze with electronic markers is obtaining the newest programming. Several companies have sprung up over the past few years specializing in the supply of aftermarket chips and gun-control programming. Some markers can have new programs installed over the Internet or through *flashing* (re-programming an existing chip), while others require the replacement of the entire circuit board. Costs for these new programs range from free (upgraded software from the manufacturer is sometimes included as part of the warranty) to a couple of hundred dollars for custom code. Most boards and re-programming tend to be in the $75 to $150 range.

The purpose of the program codes inside an electronic marker is to control the various electronic gadgets that operate the marker. Most electronic markers have a microswitch located behind the trigger and a solenoid that activates the sear. Pulling the trigger sends power to the solenoid, firing the marker. However, the program may instruct the marker to cycle three times for every trigger pull, or to fire continuously until the trigger is released.

Other (generally higher end) electronic markers incorporate an electronic valving mechanism and a *breech sensor* of some kind, and require more programming to operate. In these kinds of markers, the program may prevent the marker from firing if there is no ball loaded in the breech (the breech sensor, usually a form of electronic eye, sends a ball-loaded or ball-not-loaded signal to the chip). The program also controls how long the valve remains open for each shot (called *dwell*) and how fast the marker cycles (called *rate of fire*). Some electronically control gas input pressure, send signals to the loader telling it when to feed a new ball into the breech, and others include nifty user displays that contain game timers, rate of fire, number of shots fired, battery life indicators and a whole panoply of video-game like features.

To complicate matters further, many tournament circuits have their own rules governing rate of fire issues and may or may not allow different kinds of firing *modes*. For example, one league requires players to manually activate their marker three times, after which the marker is allowed to fire as fast as it can. Another league does not allow any kind of electronic assistance for the rate of fire at all. These firing modes (mode to a paintballer) are tweaked and sweated over by programming geniuses attempting to find the most efficient way to max out the performance of a marker.

There are also quite a few illegal or cheater boards on the market, so a little research with the tournament league, scenario game, or field of your choice is necessary before investing in aftermarket programming.

HOW GAS TANKS WORK

Most tanks these days have *pin valves*, which operate in virtually the same fashion as the valve on a bicycle or automobile tire. A stem inside the valve has a seal on one end and a spring at the same end that causes the seal to close off the tank valve. When you screw the tank into the adapter on the marker, a nub inside the adapter depresses the pin, causing the valve to open, allowing gas to flow from the tank and into the valve of the marker.

All tanks come with a pressure-relief valve called a *burst disk*. (Some tanks that come supplied with a regulator have more than one burst disk—a high-pressure burst disk for the volume of gas stored in the tank and a low- pressure burst disk attached to the output (low-pressure) side of the regulator.)

The burst disk is an essential piece of safety equipment; servicing of a burst disk is best left to a trained individual. Essentially, the burst disk consists of four parts—a nut (usually with a hexagonal head), a gas passage bored through the body of the nut, a pressure disk, and a seal. The nut closes off an opening into the tank. The pressure disk is a thin piece of copper designed to fail when the pressure inside the tank reaches unsafe levels. Once the pressure disk fails, gas is vented out through the passage in the nut, allowing the pressure in the tank to be relieved in a safe and controlled manner.

Fixing a tank that has *blown a disk* is a simple matter of unscrewing the used (and now useless) burst disk nut and replacing it with a new one. However, *a word of caution* here: proper installation of a burst disk requires the proper selection of the appropriate burst disk and the correct amount of torque on the nut. Since tank safety ultimately rests with the burst disk, it's best to spend the few dollars ($2 to $10) to get it properly serviced and installed.

HOW REGULATORS WORK

A *regulator* is a pressure adjuster, a device to regulate the pressure that is allowed to flow out of a tank. Most regulators used with paintball are of the spring-operated type. The spring inside a regulator requires a certain amount of force to become compressed; when that amount of force from the pressurized gas is applied to a pin attached to the spring, the regulator opens and allows gas to flow. Basically, the pressure of the gas is used to push open the valve. Adjustable regulators control the amount of force needed by adjusting the amount of tension placed on the regulator spring.

HOW LOADERS WORK

The operational characteristics of a gravity-feed loader are pretty straightforward. Balls are held in a storage area that has an opening to a port or neck. Natural forces (gravity, the fact that balls roll) cause the paintballs to move towards the outlet in the neck. Playing action, the firing of the gun, and recoil contribute to jostling the balls so that there is a continuous flow from the storage area into the neck, and through the neck into the breech of the marker.

Force-feed loaders start with a storage area similar in shape and design to a gravity loader. Each force-feed system then employs one of several methods for detecting whether or not a ball is in the neck of the loader, ready to drop into the breech. These mechanisms are such things as vibration sensors, reed switches, or electronic eyes. In most cases, the absence of a paintball in the proper position is sensed by the electronic mechanism, which sends a signal to a circuit board that then activates the feed mechanism. Feed mechanisms run from the sublime to the surrealistic: a small motor with weedwacker cord attached spins to jostle balls into the feed neck, or an extremely complicated system of gears and baffles forces balls into a rotary tray, that then pushes balls into the neck.

There are other systems, but the above provides a general review of how the majority of these systems work.

In operation, a force-feed loader is first turned on; where provided, the sensitivity of the sensing mechanism is adjusted and the speed of operation (expressed as *balls per second*) is adjusted. Once attached to a gun, the cycling of the breech will cause a ball to fall through the feed neck, activating and/or deactivating the sensor, which causes the force-feed mechanisms to operate. Some loaders can be wired directly into the marker, allowing the gun's own programming to control the loader's operation. Some markers work better with one model loader, others with a different make, so it's best to check what the manufacturer recommends.

HOW PAINTBALLS WORK

Paintballs are extremely fine pieces of engineering. Consider: a liquid filled capsule goes from 0 to 300 feet per second in just ten inches of travel, sails through the air, slowing down all the while, and then breaks against a soft target. That paintball has to be strong enough to withstand being shot out of a gun, yet fragile enough to break when it hits, even when traveling at half of its original speed.

The balls are manufactured out of gelatin using a rotary encapsulation process. This process is the same as is used for creating vitamin E capsules, bath oil beads and various medications. It is also known as a soft-gel process (because the gelatin is more pliable and formable.) Hard gel—a form of gelatin also used for encapsulation—utilizes a different process.

Gelatin is created by processing animal bone, skin and other tissues, creating collagen. Using heat and mixing with other chemicals (plasticizers) a long, thin ribbon of material is created. Color is added and this is fed into an encapsulation machine.

Also running into the encapsulator is the *fill* or paint. Everyone has their own secret formula (Some formulations are patented.), but they all essentially consist of inert agents for providing color and viscosity.

The gelatin ribbons are fed over a cylindrical die (the rotary die) that has a number of hemispherical depressions located along its surface. These depressions (one half of the paintball shell) are attached to a vacuum line.

There are two opposing cylinders in the machine, with a ribbon of gelatin being fed onto each one and a fill reservoir located between them. As the cylinders (dies) rotate towards each other, they pull the gelatin sheet with them, over the pockets on its surface. A vacuum pulls the gelatin into the pocket as it passes through the fill reservoir. At this point two opposing pockets are rotated together, forming a sphere with the fill trapped between them. The two halves are sealed together and the balls drop onto a conveyer that transports them to tumbling, drying and inspection processes.

While paintballs have been carefully engineered over the years to be environmentally friendly, non-toxic and household friendly (in other words, non-permanently staining), there are still some problems you can run into.

Ingestion of paintballs by dogs, who seem to like the taste, is a bad thing. It was recently discovered that a chemical in paintballs can cause neurological problems in canines that can lead to death. Very little information is available about this phenomena, so until more is learned, it's best to keep the paintballs away from dogs.

Paintballs also attract insects (ants in particular), so balls being left around the house can cause bug issues. Paintballs left out on the lawn shouldn't be much of an issue—the gelatin will break down after a few heavy morning dews or rain (and/or get eaten by the previously mentioned bugs).

So far as their claims for being non-staining are concerned well, they're *mostly* true. You might want to use this opportunity to teach your kids how to do the laundry (if they haven't learned and forgotten already.)

The dye inside a paintball will permanently/semi-permanently stain the following materials:

- Expensive, man-made carpet fibers
- Drywall
- Plaster
- Stucco
- Some plastics
- Some paint sealants or overcoats (i.e., used on car finishes or wood staining/wood waterproofing treatments)
- Some nylon formulations used in clothing

Therefore, I suggest that you find an area of your house that either contains none of the above or whose appearance doesn't matter, and use that as a staging area when the kids return from a day of paintball play. A porch, a garage or a basement with an exterior entrance, are good places to start. Have the kids divest themselves of all of their paintball gear (especially their shoes) in that location before entering the house proper. That way you avoid multi-colored shoe tracks through the 6-inch-pile, all-white, shag carpet in the living room.

If you do end up having a staining accident, try to clean it up as quickly as possible. (For example, paint splotches on the car will leave no lasting mark if cleaned off in the first half hour or so)—but don't use methods that will spread the stain. Dab instead of wipe. Use cleaning supplies appropriate to the surface material in question.

Paint will readily come off of most modern wallpapers, countertop surfaces, latex paints, ceramics, glass, plastics and metals. It will also wash out of most fibers—although you may have to apply a stain stick and put the article in question through a few cycles. When it comes to cleaning paint off of just about anything, the sooner you get to it, the easier and more effective the cleaning will be.

There are a few staining fill-formulations on the market (mostly found in cheap paintballs or high-end, no-wipe, tournament-grade paintballs). These are usually found in bright pink, orange and yellow fills, and more often than not contain iodine. The industry has banned these formulations, but some are still floating around.

Finally, if your back yard is being used as a playing field, be aware that the trees and bushes will probably show some staining (a whitish discoloration on bark) for awhile, but, unless staining fills are being used, these will wash off after a good rain or two.

CHAPTER 4:
<u>PAINTBALL AND HEALTH CONCERNS</u>

MEDICAL CONSIDERATIONS

Medically speaking, your concerns as a parent should be the same concerns you'd have for any other outdoor recreational activity. Your child should be: physically capable of moving around the field, able to engage in activity that will heighten cardio-vascular activity, properly attired for the environment, and properly equipped for the expected weather conditions.

For example, players should be encouraged to wear footgear that incorporates ankle support because they'll be doing a lot of stop-and-go running. If the weather is hot, they should have a good supply of water and/or sports drinks readily available. If they are prone to allergies, the proper medication should be on hand.

If your child is taking *any* prescription medication, you should consult with your family physician to insure that participating in paintball won't interfere with the medication or that the medication will preclude play.

When it comes to injury, beyond everyday recreational activity injuries (cuts, scrapes, abrasion burns, insect bites, sprained joints), there are a few things to be aware of.

First, paintball impacts cause bruises and welts. While these can look horrible, most people don't have a problem with them. Most are subcutaneous (below the skin) and will go through the usual spreading and color changes you'll see from any bruise. (Most players like to show off their welts as badges of honor; they usually don't hurt at all except for the initial impact, and may be slightly tender or sore a day or so after the game, but for the most part, it's just a small bruise.) Some people do take much longer to heal from bruises and,

105

like any injury, it's a good idea to keep an eye on them to make sure they are healing properly.

Beyond the welts, there are really only three possible major medical issues that can occur as a result of playing the game of paintball. These are—*aneurysm, concussion* and *comottio cordis.*

Aneurysm

Personally, I've only seen one case of this resulting from a paintball hit (to the head), but that only means that it can happen again, and probably has. An aneurysm is a bubble in a blood vessel that forms in a weakened section of the blood vessel wall. When they pop, they can have devastating effects. Fortunately, it is unlikely that a paintball will cause an aneurysm deep inside the body or brain where it could have fatal effects, but will rather be on the surface. If one develops, minor in-patient surgery can usually handle the problem.

Concussion

It has only recently been learned by the medical community that the effects of concussion—even from minor head bumps—last a lot longer than anyone realized. Additionally, re-injury while the brain is still healing can have wide-ranging effects seemingly out of proportion to the nature of the subsequent injury.

Most players wear some form of head protection (from a solid helmet to a woolen beanie hat), which is usually more that adequate to protect against the occasional head shot.

Concussion is, unfortunately, an all too common occurrence on the paintball field, particularly on the tournament field, where *bunkering* is common. Players who take a sharp hit to the head (or, more likely, multiple head impacts) should be encouraged to cease play for the day. They should also be monitored for several hours following the incident, and medical assistance should be obtained if they experience blurred vision, nausea, light-headedness, vertigo, ringing in the ears, appear to be unbalanced, slur their speech or appear to be generally confused and out of it.

It is a myth that you only experience a concussion if you lose consciousness, and it is now well known that recovery from a concussion takes far longer than originally believed. Furthermore, individuals who suffered a concussion are much more vulnerable to repeat concussions while they are going through the recovery process.

Commotio Cordis

This has only recently come to the attention of sports medicine through several highly publicized incidents from around the country involving baseball. Essentially, a sharp blow to the chest at precisely the correct time can apparently interrupt the body's electrical control of the heart and respiratory system, causing them to stop, with fatal results. Youngsters are apparently more vulnerable to this than adults, but it remains a little understood phenomena. To date, no one is aware of any cases occurring during the play of paintball, but it has been seen on the baseball and basketball fields. It may be that paintballs do not possess enough mass to strike a heavy enough blow, but some medical personnel associated with paintball have brought it to everyone's attention as a possible concern. It is also apparently not amenable to solutions such as using chest protectors—the "shockwave" of the impact being transmitted through such padding—so, for right now, the best defense is the knowledge that this can occur.

Please also be aware that overly padding your child to protect them from paintball hits is almost a guarantee that they will be shot at excessively during a game. It's one of the facts of paintball life that, in order to play, you have to take the hit—which roughly translates into *if you can't stand the heat, get out of the kitchen.* Excessive padding is perceived by more experienced players as a red flag that says "this player can't take the hit," and the inevitable result is that they take it upon themselves to show the player that the padding doesn't really do them much good. While many companies in the industry make chest protectors, wearing one marks the player as weak. So, a word to the wise: if you or your child insists on a chest protector—wear it *under* a layer of clothing.

Allergies and Asthma

Any player who has allergies or asthma should be prepared with their medication and other support systems before going to play, since paintball is a major aerobic workout, and more often than not, players will be in the woods where allergens, bees, wasps and other potentially harmful creatures abound. If your child really needs an inhaler, or is severely allergic to bee stings, it would be best if you made the field officials aware of this situation and made adequate preparations.

CHAPTER 5:
HOW PAINTBALL IS PLAYED

RULES OF THE GAME

One of the greatest things about paintball is its versatility. Like tag (a very simple concept), it can be modified and adapted in an unlimited number of ways. In fact, paintball can probably best be described as long-range tag; virtually anything you can imagine doing with a game of tag, you can adapt to a game of paintball.

There are many wonderful resources available that describe game variations—among them being *Durty Dan's Game Variations* (http://www.luminet.net/~tyger/paintball/Games/dansplat.html. This site is provided by Rob 'Tyger' Rubin, a long-time writer and videographer of the sport). I encourage players to try as many different variations as they can, because you never know what's going to turn into a great game of paintball.

When it comes to more formal versions of the game, there are a number of official rulebooks, most associated with the major leagues that support competitive play. Fortunately, all of the basic rules are very similar.

Here's a generic run down of the rules of play for *Basic Flag-based Games.*

- Designate a playing area and mark off its outer boundaries in some visible manner (surveyor's tape is the go-to solution).
- Place a starting location (flag station) at either end of the playing area.
- Place a flag station in the middle of the playing area.
- Place a flag in the center flag station (such as a towel, rag, traffic cone…); alternatively, place one flag in each of

the flag stations at the ends of the field.

- Divide players up into two teams.
- Set a time limit for the game (3 minutes, 5 minutes, 30 minutes).

To win the game, one team must take possession of the flag from the center flag station and carry it in to the opposing team's flag station—or—one team must capture the opposing team's flag and return it to their own flag station.

Players are eliminated from the game when they are hit with a paintball that breaks and leaves a mark. Players who leave the field boundary are also eliminated, as are players who voluntarily surrender (instead of getting shot).

A player who has a paintball mark on them may not be the player to hang the flag in a flag station.

Players who wipe off a paintball mark or continue to play the game with a known mark on them are considered to be cheating.

If time expires without a flag being hung or if all players on both teams are eliminated from the game (possible as a result of "simultaneous elimination"), the game ends without a winner. You can also score a game that ends without a hang of the flag by counting eliminations, by giving a win to a team that has grabbed a flag but not hung it, by the team that was the closest to hanging, etc.

Of course, many players are not interested in formal rules, aren't interested in setting up flag stations or anything like that. All they want to do is run around in the woods, shooting their guns and getting shot at, which is a perfectly acceptable way to play the game. For these style games, the simplest rules are the best, and those are found in a game variation generally referred to as *elimination*.

Rules for Elimination Games

- Designate a playing area.
- Designate starting locations.
- Divide players into two teams.
- Start the game.
- Players are eliminated from the game when they are hit.
- The first team to eliminate all of the opposing players wins.

Another popular and simple variation is called *attack and defend* or *defender*. In this variation, a small group of players is given a specific area of the playing field that they must remain within and defend, while a larger group of players attacks. This variation usually has a time limit as well.

Many other variations abound: *Zombie* is a game where anyone shot immediately joins the shooter's team. *Terminator* is a game where one or more players are essentially invincible. *Punish* is a game in which none of the hits count for an elimination until you want them to.

I'm sure that you've begun to get the picture that paintball can be played in any manner the participants agree on—and that's just fine because the whole objective is to have a good time.

A Note On Rules And Officiating

The rules for competition and scenario games have become very formal over the years and provide a lot of detail concerning equipment, *legal* hits and penalties for breaking the rules. Most of these are not appropriate for casual play, but they should be looked into nevertheless. You can't know at this stage where your son or daughter will end up in their paintball playing career and, while it might not be appropriate for casual play, they can provide some good concepts for general play.

It's also true that as players participate more frequently, they'll want more control over their games, and these rules can help them gain that control. A few important aspects of the rules are described below:

Hit Size. Most players generally agree that a little bit of splash from a near hit shouldn't count. Most players also agree that a direct hit, as long as it leaves a little paint, should count. Over the years, we've settled on "hits the size of a quarter or larger" are good for elimination. It's generally good to agree on a size before play begins so everyone is on the same page.

Hit Distance. Many people limit the distance that someone can be shot from to increase safety. This ranges anywhere from 4 to 20 feet. While this looks like a good idea at the beginning, it usually ends up causing arguments over exactly how far away someone was when shooting. It also ends up teaching bad playing skills, so I personally recommend against distance rules. (Most national events do not utilize distance rules; learning to play with such rules can put the player at a disadvantage.)

Surrender Rules. To minimize close range shooting, many people also use surrender rules. Essentially this involves a player asking for another player to surrender when they are within some minimum distance of each other. The best variation on this rule is the black and white one: if the player being offered a surrender doesn't immediately lower their gun, they get shot. This minimizes confusion and prevents a player from holding up the game by hemming and hawing over a surrender decision. It also protects the player offering the surrender from a "spin and shoot" by the surrenderer. (Again, generally not used in competitive play, and therefore usage results in improper playing skills.)

Playing On. Playing on is the act of continuing to play with a legitimate hit on your body. Oftentimes this is accidental (a player is marked somewhere they can't see or feel), but it is also the most popular method of "cheating." Without referees to control the situation, it's left up to the players to administer justice. My recommendation is a stern warning, and then, if the player persists in playing this way, refusing to allow them to participate.

Officiating. Most people want to play a fair game. When not at a commercial facility, the best way to do this is to have the first couple of players to be eliminated turn into game officials. This keeps things generally fair, since no one knows who is going to get eliminated first. (Of course, if players are abusing their officiating privileges, it's time to come up with a different solution.)

Signaling Elimination. It's very difficult to tell an eliminated player from a live player, and so best to have a formal method of signaling when someone is no longer in the game. The generally accepted method these days is for the eliminated player to shout—once— "OUT" or "HIT," put their barrel blocking device on their marker and then raise it into the air, over their head, as they walk off the playing area. Please note that it is not at all unusual for an eliminated player to continue to receive hits after they have indicated they are out. This is due to several factors, amongst which are—not hearing the signal, not seeing the signal, multiple balls in the air already, multiple shooters firing at the player. It is counterintuitive, but the best way to avoid "bonus balls" (extra hits after being eliminated) is to stand up as quickly as possible with the gun in the air while yelling "HIT!" Players who hide or curl up to avoid the extra hits are perceived as either uneliminated players or players who are trying to cheat; instead of stopping the shots from coming in, these actions usually *increase* the volume of fire.

Limiting Target Areas. Some players limit the areas of the body and equipment that count for an elimination. Some use *elbows and knees* (where anything below the knees or elbows doesn't count); some use *equipment doesn't count* (hits on guns or loaders); some use *head shots don't count* and others use *torso only* (where only hits on the chest, abdomen or back count). All of these can help players stay in a game longer and, if used in a limited fashion, can help players learn when they are exposing themselves to being hit, but in most cases they leave the player unable to participate in games that don't have these rules. I also strongly recommend against *head shots don't count* because it has been demonstrated time and again that, rather than reducing the instances of hits on the head, this rule actually increases the number of head shots. Players tend to leave their heads exposed when this rule is in effect and, since hits there don't count, opposing players use them for target practice.

Equipment Limitations. Most players quickly learn to limit the amount of padding allowed in a game. Normal protective gear is acceptable; pillows, foam rubber, and winter parkas are not. They are also fairly sensitive to gun technology limitations and self-limit what versions players can and can't use. In general, high rate-of-fire markers should not be used against pump guns or low rate-of-fire markers, or, at the least, the mix of technology should be evenly spread between the teams participating. I recommend against allowing everyone to use full-auto rates of fire for two simple reasons: full-auto is *expensive* in paint and it can get dangerous out there with so much paint flying. Full-auto is also almost universally banned from formal play because of safety considerations.

Most of the rulebooks for various competition play are available on the web. Most of them are based on a single set of rules I developed for the National Professional Paintball League in 1992. You can find out where to obtain copies of these rules, as well as scenario game rules and game variations in the appendices.

PLAYING AT COMMERCIAL FIELDS

If you've come this far, your darling child is going to be playing some paintball. Fantastic! Let's make sure that both you and your child make the most of this first experience.

It's now time to pick up the phone (or get your kid off their lazy butt and have them do it) and start calling around to the local commercial establishments. There are a bunch of questions you'll want to ask, and we'll go over the whys and wherefores below.

The first thing you should know is that commercial paintball operations come in all types. Truly impressive operations exist out there—some that have hundreds of acres of playing land, modern facilities, the latest in field layouts and decades of operational experience, and then there are others being run by Billy-Joe-Bob out of the back of his pickup truck.

Don't immediately assume that Billy-Joe-Bob's operation is bad and the expensive looking place is good. Billy-Joe-Bob might just have the lowest prices around, some of the best terrain anyone has ever seen, and a well-trained professional staff. An experience at a commercial playing site has more to do with customer service and professionalism than it does with facilities—just like most any other outdoor entertainment you might participate in.

There are, however, certain things you want to see from any field (safety consciousness being key among them) that, if not present, can turn the best field in the world into the worst paintball experience ever.

Fields come in three general types—*woodsball, concept,* and *indoor* (with indoor fields generally breaking down into *maze* style and *concept* style).

A woodsball field is just what it sounds like—a paintball

115

field where games take place in the woods.

The woods are where it all began for paintball, so playing in the woods is probably still the best training and learning environment for any new paintball player. *All* of the skills learned while playing woodsball are useful on any other kind of field, while skills learned only on the concept fields are mostly only useful for concept field play.

Woodsball fields with a wide variety of terrain offer an almost unlimited number of playing experiences, as games in a pine forest are far different from play on sand dunes or play in a swamp, or play along a streambed or on hilly terrain.

Concept fields are the second generation of playing sites and feature man-made obstacles and terrain, typically *inflatables* (large, balloon-like structures of different shapes and sizes), pallets, spools, and various structures made of wood or plastic. These fields offer faster play, the ability to watch and analyze games, and have become the accepted standard for competition play.

Indoor fields have run the gamut from the original maze designs (very close quarters, many doors, windows, blind angles, etc) to fully enclosed concept fields; there have also been several attempts to bring the woods indoors using artificial trees and shrubs.

Indoor fields tend to be most popular in areas where the climate is not conducive to outdoor play and where there are opportunities to offer nighttime play; while many events have been held inside large indoor stadiums, indoor fields are not nearly as popular with players, nor are they anywhere near as common as the other types of fields.

Most well managed fields offer a variety of field types these days so that they can cater to differing customer desires. A really good facility is one that offers both concept fields and woodsball, varying terrain, different styles of concept fields, and on-location product and technical support. This type of field can most often be found near large metropolitan areas.

It may be a personal bias of mine, but I would suggest starting play at anything but an indoor field. It's not that indoor fields are bad, just that most indoor fields are restrictive in size and the terrain rarely changes from day to day, giving the locals who play there frequently a major advantage. Playing for the first time on a field where others have an advantage is detrimental to learning the game.

When researching a field, you'll need to call and ask the following questions:

Questions To Ask When Calling A Field

- *What are the days/hours of operation?*

Most fields are open on the weekends; some have weekday and evening hours as well.

- *Do they have rental equipment?*

Most do, for a fee.

- *What kind of rental equipment is available?*

Most rental gear is of the low-end variety; some fields offer *upgrades* for a higher fee, which will make your child more competitive in the equipment department.

- *Is there a good time for a novice to attend?*

Some fields have days or hours devoted to new players, but most do not. Some fields (many of them in fact) have special times when the more experienced players attend to hold practices and scrimmages—which you want to avoid.

- *Do they have insurance coverage?*

Most fields do, but some work on a *self-insured waiver* program, meaning that they do not have a liability policy. Whether to attend such a field is up to you, but it is not that uncommon these days and the real decision ought to be based on how safely they run their operation.

- *Do they have telephone service out at the field?*

117

A little unusual to ask, but many fields are out in the sticks and might not have a decent communication set-up.

- *How many games will players get to play?*

Most fields will offer multiple hours of play with no set number of games, but it would be nice to hear that they try to give everyone between six and ten (or more) games in a four+ hour session.

- *What is your usual attendance?*

The bottom line is that many well run, regularly operated paintball fields have days of good attendance and days of bad or no attendance—and you want your kid to have lots of targets to shoot at.

As you talk to the owner or manager of the field in question, you will undoubtedly gain a feel for them; if they sound fly-by-night, unsure of themselves, wishy-washy, or arrogant, I'd suggest taking your business elsewhere.

Most places around the country are fortunate enough to have several playing facilities within a given area—it will be the rare player who won't have more than one field to choose from. A good place to find fields is www.pbreview.com—they have a whole section devoted to field reviews organized by state. Take the reviews with a grain of salt; good reviews are often padding written by employees and friends and bad reviews are sometimes written by competitors.

Your next step is to do a reconnaissance of the facility. Don't plan on participating—you're just going to check out the lay of the land, the other customers, the facilities and confirm pricing information.

Paintball can be played just about anywhere; the legions of backyard 'ballers will be happy to inform you that you don't need a dedicated facility to play, so don't make a snap judgment about the facilities you visit. Plan on spending a little time (steeling yourself against the inevitable begging that you'll be hearing from your kid who wants to play), and to do a good review, spend some time.

The primary thing you'll want to be on the lookout for is the enforcement of safety rules. You'll want to see an adequate number of staff, enclosed areas where goggles can be removed, good separation of the fields themselves from parking and other non-playing areas, well-kept and clean facilities, and customers who are obviously having a good time.

What you don't want to see are the following:

- Players on fields without supervision
- Game officials (referees) who are not being effective, don't appear to know what they are doing, or seem intimidated by the players
- Game officials who act rude, discourteous or unprofessional
- Players who blatantly ignore safety regulations, roughhouse inappropriately, display bad manners, engage in physical or verbal intimidation, or generally misbehave
- Facilities maintained in an unsafe manner; field netting with holes in it, man-made bunkers that are sharp with nails or screws exposed, ground litter that could be harmful, inappropriate boundary markers around fields
- Inadequate sanitation facilities and generally unsafe conditions

The vast majority of paintball fields are *works in progress*. Don't let the appearance put you off. Some really well run fields look like hellholes, but that's because they're supposed to. For example, there used to be a field outside of Chicago that had cars scattered all over it; they were rusty, discolored and looked bad, until you realized that all of the glass had been removed, all of the locks had been removed, trunks and hoods had been permanently sealed closed, and there were no exposed surfaces that could injure someone. Watching players on the field, it quickly became obvious that they enjoyed using it.

It truly is the people who make or break a good paintball facility, and it is the people in charge—owner, manager, game officials—who you should be watching, questioning and analyzing when choosing a field.

A Note About The Other Players

There are not, unfortunately, enough regular players enjoying this game to allow a field the luxury of specializing in one type of player. Almost every field has to cater to and provide facilities for the vast range of potential customers out there—everyone from the total neophyte to the professionally-sponsored competition player.

This can have unfortunate consequences for the newer player in a number of ways. Quite frequently, players of widely varying experience and talent are placed on a field together, either on the same or opposite teams. This can work out to an inexperienced player's benefit, but unfortunately, here's what usually happens:

The local team or tournament wannabe players all end up on one side and beat the heck out of the newbies.

The experienced player gets bent out of shape—either because the newbie is at fault for losing the game or because the newbie "must have cheated" to have been able to eliminate such an overwhelmingly experienced player.

There is obviously no excuse for this type of behavior. It is, unfortunately, common enough that this kind of player has earned his own nickname, the *TWiB* or *tournament wannabe*. The TwiB is an arrogant SOB, foul-mouthed, disrespectful and of the general opinion that no one else on the field deserves to win a game, let alone eliminating them on the field. Since they have no real tournament abilities, acting this way is their only real opportunity to win at paintball.

Many people think that TwiBs are actual professional players (TwiBs also tend to lie a lot about who they play for, how good they are and how much industry support and sponsorship they receive.). *Most* professional players (no one yet makes their living entirely by playing) are people who love the sport and are freely giving of their time and experience. They've been painted with a broad brush, though, since they are highly visible. Most of them don't waste their time playing against inexperienced or recreational players. When they do, it's usually in a clinic or training setting. The bad actors are usually players on lesser teams who think that they are supposed to act out and be arrogant.

Because of these kinds of players, it's best to see for yourself if the field allows what those in the industry call newbie bashing—the practice of allowing experienced players to shoot up the inexperienced. Don't be fooled by the excuses. You may hear that the new players want to do it, or that it's a good way to learn how to play.

New players do want to play against these people—until after the game is over in about 30 seconds.

It would be a good way to learn—if it lasted long enough to learn something.

Under controlled circumstances, players need to play against those who are better than they are—the key being *control.*

Believe me, you'll quickly learn to tell a good field—one that cares for each and every customer and caters to individual needs—from a bad field. And remember that every sport and activity has its bad actors, but you and your child don't have to be stuck playing with them.

HOW THE DAY WILL GO

Your child will show up at the field during operating hours, cash or credit card in hand, filled with a lot of excitement, anticipation, fear and trepidation. Whether you drop your child off and let them fend for themselves or you stay and help support them is up to you—but you just might want to hang around for a couple of hours to watch all of the fun.

Once at the field, your child will be asked to pay their entry fee, their *fill fee*, and will be asked if they wish to purchase paint. (Some fields will charge a separate fee for rental equipment, and some fields will include paint, air, lunch or some combination thereof with the entry fee.)

Players who purchase an *air card* or *all day air* will receive some kind of sticker, wrist band or other form of receipt that will allow them to obtain these services without paying additional fees throughout the day. (Except in rare circumstances, an all-day-air card is a good bargain.)

Most players will purchase anywhere from 500 to 2000 paintballs at this point (expect that your kid will be needing the same). (Some fields are *FPO*—Field Paint Only, others are *BYOP*—Bring Your Own Paint, and still others are both, selling paint and allowing customers to bring their own in for a small surcharge.) Since this is your child's first time out—I'd purchase the field paint, even if the field allows you to bring in your own.

Once the fees are paid, the field will present an insurance waiver to be signed; minor children will need a parent or guardian to sign a separate permission section of the waiver. (Please note that many fields now have their waivers and parental permission forms on-line, and most that don't will be happy to fax or email the form to you so that you can fill it out in advance.)

The waivers run the gamut from a simple sign-in sheet to two-page legal monstrosities. They all serve one purpose, and that is to get you to acknowledge that playing paintball may result in injuries they don't want to be responsible for.

This shouldn't concern you if you've checked the field out already—but I'd still read through the fine print. The bottom line on waivers is this: when paintball is played responsibly, there is little or no chance of an injury beyond those you'll see with any other recreational activity (scrapes, bruises, twisted ankles…) and no piece of paper is a shield against negligence and stupidity. The last time you visited an amusement park, I'll bet you didn't know that accepting an admission ticket also acknowledged your acceptance of the park's waiver of certain liabilities. Litigation, liability, and protecting yourself from the same have become unfortunate standards of doing business these days. As long as the field does a decent job of promoting and enforcing the safety standards (something you should already have checked out), there's no need to sweat the waiver.

Everyone will then be given a safety briefing that will stress the use of goggles and barrel blocking devices, the methods players will use to signal that they have been eliminated, the rules of the game, and a description of the games that will be played. *Now* is the time to ask questions, if there are any.

Most good fields will then let players take their markers over to a target range and get used to firing their guns. Caution your child not to go crazy at the target range; they may be having a good time, but the field owner is having a better one watching nickels fly out of the barrel every time a gun is fired.

Teams will be selected (or the group will break up into its pre-determined teams), the players will take the field and the first game will begin.

If you stay to watch and encourage, here are the three most common rookie mistakes to watch out for:

- *Failure to communicate.* Players need to talk and pass information back and forth during a game—if only to find out what is going on, whether they can move, whom they can shoot at. Most new players believe that talking will give them away and are reluctant to say anything. A good solution is to pick one other player to buddy up with, and work together, even if all they say to each other the first few times is "do you see anything?"

• *Tunnel vision.* This is the act of focusing all of your attention on a single target. Most new players think that the player directly in front of them is their worst enemy— when in fact that is the last player on the field they really need to worry about; opponents to their flanks are a worse threat, and the only way to be aware of them is to watch the entire field, all the time.

• *Lack of aggression.* Players who hide behind bunkers never get into the game. To play effectively, let alone win, players have to take calculated risks: "when in doubt, run it out"—which basically means—go and get the other team before they get you. Play offensively, not defensively.

CHAPTER 6:
PLAYING TIPS

BASIC SKILLS TO MASTER/MISTAKES TO AVOID

I can't possibly include all of the skills, tips, tricks and tactical moves necessary for a good paintballer to know. There are many fine training videos, other books, magazine articles, and clinics devoted to just that subject (many of which you'll find referenced in the Appendices), but I can give you a few insights that can make you sound like a paintball know-it-all.

Earlier, I referenced the three most common rookie mistakes—*Failure to Communicate*, *Tunnel Vision*, and *Failure to Play Aggressively*. Here are some tips for learning how to avoid these mistakes:

For communications—Learn each player's name on your team. Players respond more easily when their names are called. Go on to the field with two or three things that you will say or ask continuously during the course of the game, such as "Frank, what do you have?" (asking Frank what he sees on the field) or "Billy, what's the count?" (asking Billy how many opponents have been eliminated). Also, learn to update your teammates with your condition: "He's on me," means an opponent is shooting at your position. "Dorito is hot," means that there is an opponent in the Dorito bunker (or whatever type of bunker the opponent is in). Also, try to remember to repeat, loudly, any other meaningful communication that is transmitted by other teammates, such as the count, an elimination call (Most players know that a call of "D1!"—or something similar—means an opponent was just eliminated, so repeat it.). Finally, it doesn't hurt to have a "nonsense" call—something you can yell when you need or want to yell something to keep the talk going. Anything that won't be confused with true game

125

information will do, even a "woohoo!" works.

For tunnel vision—If your child is driving, this is an easy one. Treat the playing field like it was your car; check the dash, the rearview mirror, the side-view mirrors, and then the windshield—and keep repeating the routine. Keep in mind that it is not necessary to point your gun everywhere you are looking; if you have a known target, keep the marker on them while looking around. (It also helps to start developing a healthy *sixth-sense*. If the hairs on the back of your neck start going up and you have a feeling that something is about to happen—*pay attention*! If the feeling is to move—do it. If the feeling is to look somewhere else, do it. None of us know how this works—maybe we're subconsciously picking up on clues—but work it does, and every good player learns to develop and trust this skill.

For developing proper aggression—Don't be afraid to get eliminated. It's as simple as that. Once you get eliminated, sit back and analyze the situation. Did you get hit because you weren't aware of a player's location? Did you get hit because you tried to move too far? Did you get hit because you didn't take proper cover? Keep trying the same aggressive moves until you get them sorted out successfully. Proper aggression also means proper follow-thru—completing the move. Stopping short on a run usually guarantees elimination.

Other playing tips

- Once the game starts, *never* lower your gun; always keep it up and ready to fire.
- Learn how to shoot with your "weak-side" hand; a player presents a smaller profile when shooting left-handed on the left side of cover and right-handed from the right side of cover.
- Don't ever put just one shot on a target—rip on it.

- Learn to lean out of cover rather than stepping out from it—only the portion of your body necessary to clear the bunker should move.
- Learn to snapshoot—a quick pop out from behind cover, 1 to 3 shots and then back into cover.
- Always change your shooting position—especially if you are duking it out with an opponent. Shoot from the right of cover, from the top, from the left. Don't let them get a fix on your location.
- Learn to run—fast—while crouched over.
- Learn to dive and slide.
- Make sure you keep an eye on the paint in your hopper and reload *before* you need to.
- Learn how to play different kinds of bunkers. Sometimes tucking in very tight to a bunker is the right way to play it; other times playing off the bunker (back a few feet) is the proper move. Learn to analyze shooting situations so you play the bunker correctly.
- Target shoot! The marker is the primary tool of the paintballer and it should be mastered.

CHAPTER 7:
NON-COMMERCIAL PLAY

PLAYING IN THE BACKYARD

Playing in the backyard is a relatively new phenomenon and has become so common that it is believed by the industry that anywhere from 2/3 to 3/4 of all play takes place on private land.

It wasn't until very recently that the necessary equipment, supplies, and availability of same even made it possible to consider playing anywhere except on a commercial field.

It's only fair of me to state before going any farther that I'm not personally a big fan of backyard play—and here's why:

Lack of Community. Backyard players form small groups whose only participation in the world of paintball is to purchase product off the web, or from a single local supplier (who in many cases is not a legitimate business). This is usually good for pricing issues, but generally bad for safety, definitely bad for playing skills, and limits the player's ability to gain knowledge about the sport. To put it another way, small local groups tend to in-breed. If no one in the group is educated in the safety requirements, the *group* is uneducated. Methods of play are limited and therefore player skills are stunted or non-existent.

Lack of Skills. When players are not challenged by more knowledgeable and skillful players, their own abilities are not stretched. They begin to play in a standard manner—always making the same moves, always facing the same opponents, always playing on the same terrain in the same manner. Eventually, this gets old and boring, and players lose their interest in the game.

Perpetuation of Bad Myths. One player in a small group

finds some new thing they can do with paintball (for example, freezing paintballs), passes it on to the group and everyone starts doing it—because there's no one there with greater knowledge and experience to explain why this might be a bad idea.

Lack of Responsibility. Again, since there is no connection to paintball as a whole, there's no incentive to engage in safe, wholesome activities and nothing to put the breaks on bad, irresponsible behavior. If a small group gets it in their head to shoot up cars or houses, there's no one there to explain that this will be bad for everyone who plays.

However, I do recognize that backyard play is often the only way many players can afford to participate in paintball, so, after encouraging you to visit commercial fields, I'll also encourage you to manage your backyard games as safely and responsibly as you can.

SELECTING TERRAIN AND WHERE TO PLAY

The general rule for safety around a playing field is a buffer zone of 300+ feet and/or physical obstacles a *minimum* of 12 feet high.

If you can't provide these kinds of buffers around the playing field—don't play there.

Any open field or patch of woods around which you can place such a buffer will do for a playing site (provided that the terrain itself is safe to use).

Fields can be inexpensively marked with surveyor's tape by running a line of tape all around the boundary of the field (tied off to trees or stakes).

The number *one* rule about using terrain is *having permission.*

If you own the property—great. For public land, you'll need to obtain permission from the local/state/federal authorities responsible for it. If it's a friend's or relatives piece of land—ask, and make sure you inform them of the following:

If they give permission for you to use the land to play, they may be responsible for dealing with insurance claims as a result of injuries.

Backyard play may be cheaper than commercial play, but if you're going to do it right, you've still got to do most of the things that commercial field operators do.

If you are using your own property, check your homeowners' insurance policy. Chances are you'll find that injuries resulting from playing paintball are *not* covered by the policy, since most insurance companies will try to make the case that you were conducting a commercial activity.

If you're using the woods, whether it's your own property or not, find out if it's used for hunting and pay attention to the hunting season. Deer hunters wear safety orange for a reason. Paintball players in the woods try to hide, so a deer hunter versus a paintball player is a losing proposition for the paintballer. Listening to buckshot whistle through the trees is pretty cool, but not when it's aimed at you...

Also, don't forget that friendly agreements between individuals ("Don't worry, I won't ever sue you,") often fall apart in the face of major medical expenses, family and attorneys. It's just something else you'll need to keep in mind.

Woods fields are the easiest to find and set-up, since most of the field terrain (bunkers) is already there and all you'll really have to do is define the outer boundaries and a couple of flag stations. Open fields large enough to handle a game are not as common, but if that's what you have to work with, you'll be needing to find or make some *bunkers*.

In general, when laying out a field (woods or airball), balance and equal distribution of terrain is what you are looking for. If the terrain is hilly, don't put one station at the top of the hill and one at the bottom—put both mid-way up the hill and play across the hill. If there is a stream running through the terrain, try to put both flag stations an equal distance from it. Try to equally distribute rough terrain, or balance out an area of heavy terrain with a much larger area of lighter terrain.

Use the surveyors' tape to mark off field boundaries and flag stations (a triangle of trees being most commonly used); use more tape to mark off areas you don't want to use (a steep cliff, a known hornets' nest…). If the woods are thick and the area is large, it would also be a good idea to mark off paths that lead back to your staging area (the set up area everyone assembles in prior to the start of a game). Mark off trees with a different color tape in a path from the field to the entrance/exit. Lost players can be instructed to look for the trees marked with that color tape and follow the path out of the woods.

Bunkers in the woods are usually pretty easy to make. Gather up the larger branches lying on the ground and use them to construct obstacles. One effective method is to use four branches stuck into the ground like fence posts (two branches a few inches apart, a long gap and then another set of two branches a few inches apart) and then stack other branches between them. You can also use existing deadfalls, or dig shallow pits, piling up the excavated dirt as a berm to increase the coverage.

If you are using an open field, you can always purchase a set of bunkers from one of several manufacturers (with a small field ranging anywhere from $1200 to $2500), or you can use construction site leavings. Old doors, wire spools, tires, shipping pallets, discarded furniture—you name it, it can be used.

Be aware that anything you use for a bunker should be inspected for exposed nails, staples and screws, jagged edges, rot, insect and animal life, before being placed on the field; for general health reasons, try and insure that none of your obstacles will collect water—tires are notorious for that. You don't want to become the area's largest mosquito breeder.

EQUIPMENT FOR BACKYARD PLAY

You *should* have the following on hand:
- A hand-held chronograph. Everyone playing should have their velocity checked periodically during the day to ensure safe velocities.
- A small medical kit (snake bite, insect stings, band aids, antiseptic cream, bandages).
- A method of communication, such as a cell phone
- Cleaning supplies (paper towels, jug of water).

A fill station—either CO_2 or scuba tanks for high-pressure air—is not necessary if players have multiple tanks or a close-by source for obtaining fills. If you're far away from a store or field and want to play all day, you'll need to invest in at least one of these, and spend the time gaining a proper education in fill procedures and safety. The easiest and safest way to go is to use HPA, purchase a couple of SCUBA tanks and a *scuba fill adapter*—but this requires that all of your local players have high-pressure tanks.

Paintballs: doing a buy for the group will always be less expensive than each individual buying their own. Find a local retailer willing to work with you.

Rules for playing are available all over the net. I'm not recommending any particular form of play, just the concept that you have at least a minimal set of rules. Get them out there early, make sure everyone who plays at the field receives them and understands them, and then stick to them. This practice will go a long way towards keeping things under control, reducing arguments, and ensuring a good, safe time for all.

- Everyone will have a barrel blocking device.
- Everyone will have a set of approved paintball goggles.
- Everyone will keep the BBD on their gun until the game is set to begin.
- Everyone will put their goggles on *before* the BBDs are removed. Attendees not playing will sit or stand in a designated safe location until the game is over and the BBDs are back on the markers*.
- All markers will be tested with the chronograph *before* each game. No marker shooting over 300 feet per second will be allowed in play.
- Any player engaging in bullying, over-shooting, illegal play, using illegal equipment, misbehaving, etc., will be asked to leave and will not be welcomed back (and their parents will be called…).
- A defined method for a player to signal that they have been eliminated is described.
- A defined method for leaving the field of play is described.
- A set game time
- A set condition for winning and/or ending a game
- *No alcohol. no drugs. no tobacco. no firearms. no other weapons of any kind.* Don't let the kids begin to think that a paintball game is a good time to ignore all of the rules.

*Do not assume that *over there* or *out of the line of fire* is an adequate safe location; non-players should be behind a solid barrier if they are within 300 feet of the playing field. If worse comes to worse, get in the car, close the doors, and roll up the windows.

A *parent*, meaning at least one responsible adult, should be on hand to monitor the situation—at the very least during the first few times that the kids play. That parent will be out there to set the tone, make sure the rules are being enforced, and to reinforce or correct things until they are satisfied that the kids can handle the game themselves.

Do not assume that public land means that anyone is free to use it for whatever purpose they have in mind.

Check local ordnances for prohibitions that might affect the use of paintball guns.

Check with the local police department: *inform* the police department that children will be playing paintball at a particular location. You don't want the police responding to a "terrorists with guns" call—and believe me, it has happened before more than once.

Visit with and inform neighbors of what is going on—especially if their property borders on the playing area.

Do not let just anyone show up to play; you run the risk of operating a defacto illegal business because, unfortunately, there are players who prey on uneducated, uninformed backyard ballers. Make sure you know who your children are associating with.

Drive or stop by the site unannounced on occasion to make doubly sure the rules are being followed. If the kids know that Mom or Dad could show up at any time, they'll be more mindful of the rules and regulations.

Encourage every player to keep his or her paintball gun in a gear bag or case when traveling to and from the field. (Most uninformed people see a *gun*, not a paintball marker. I once saw 12 police officers respond with drawn guns because a local shut-in saw kids walking down the street with their paintball guns and thought her town was under attack from "the Russians." Funny, yes. Dangerous—absolutely. If nothing else is available, a pillowcase makes for an excellent gun bag (especially if it has flowers on it...)

Inform the kids of how to respond if they are approached

or confronted by police officers. The first thing they should do is (no matter how much they might disagree at the time) follow whatever instructions they are given immediately, without protest. As a civil libertarian, I personally have a major issue with writing "do whatever the police say." However, I know from personal experience that when responding to *people with guns* calls, police officers are on edge, very high on adrenaline, and have been trained to be aggressive. They will **not** stop being aggressive until *after* they feel that the current situation is under control, and they may not think it's under control until after everyone is on the ground with their hands cuffed behind them. If you protest, argue or fight back, the police officers will never get out of their mental mode of needing to get things under control and they will continue to increase the level of force and aggression they use. Once things have relaxed, quietly inform the police that you are just playing paintball, that the only guns around are paintball markers, that you have permission to be on the property you are using, and that an adult is available for them to talk to if necessary.

Make sure you have a clean-up policy in place. If someone shoots a car, a neighbor's house, whatever (accidentally, of course), they should be the ones to take responsibility and do the clean up. Acts of paintball vandalism are on the rise country-wide. Enforcing a policy of responsibility for accidental markings, safe playing behavior, and proper behavior will go a long way towards removing your children from the suspects list.

Encourage respect for wildlife. Most animals are more than happy to clear out of the area once they hear the guns going. Some may not be able to. Encountering wildlife on the field is **not** an occasion to take some free shots; everyone needs to remember that animals do not want to tangle with people. A few minutes of quiet, perhaps a little gentle encouragement, and you can safely escort the snake, bear, raccoon, deer, armadillo, or whatever out of the area. I've had face-to-face encounters will all of the above-mentioned creatures while playing and, once I showed them that there was a safe pathway out of the area, they were happy to leave of their own accord.

Think about purchasing a copy of the *Field Operator's Guide* from ProStar Labs—www.prostarsports.net—it's the number one resource for field owners and has many excellent ideas for saving money, obtaining equipment and solving problems.

THE ECONOMICS OF BACKYARD PLAY

Most players have settled on backyard play strictly from a sense of good economy. Many parents are getting in on the act too, realizing that since they are funding most of the play, the less expensive it is, the better off they are.

A typical day of play at a commercial site will run an average player anywhere from $50 to $70 dollars. Sending your kid to play once a weekend for most of the year works out to anywhere from $2000 to $3000—per child.

If you have two paintballers in the family, we're talking a serious commitment of dollars for a season of play.

Considering that you can obtain an inflatable field for under $2000, and that paintballs can be obtained for well under $40 per case (less than two cents per ball), going backyard begins to look very attractive.

SETTING UP A BACKYARD FIELD OPERATION

You'll need the land (economical only if you own it or have no-cost use), anywhere from a space 300' x 200' on up.

You'll need an inflatable field (See the appendices.).

You'll need netting (or other secure barrier around the field).

Get a chronograph (paintball velocity tester).

Have a fill station (unless there is a local facility).

The inflatable field will run anywhere from just under $1000 (for a small set) to $7500.

Netting will run a little over $1000 (poles, wire and other materials, $250- $750).

Chronographs run $75 to $300.

Fill station means $70 for adapters, a couple hundred for tanks.

Tallying it all up, you'll be spending somewhere between $2500 and $10,000.

Keeping your operation low-end, you'll find your children (you) will be saving anywhere from $20 to $50 per day of play.

If it looks like your children are going to be playing paintball for more than a single season, and you have access to land, your own backyard field might just be the way to go in order to insure that you can make the next mortgage payment!

CHAPTER 8:
COMPETITIVE PAINTBALL

PLAYING IN ORGANIZED COMPETITIONS

I hadn't been playing paintball but all of three months before I found myself captaining a team and playing in my first paintball tournament. I was lucky enough to win that first event and to take a fourth place finish in the National Competition a week later, thus getting my tournament paintball career off to a resounding start, and I ended up being heavily involved in the tournament scene from 1984 until 1997, when I retired from play.

Back then, it was possible for a completely new, uneducated and clueless team to place highly and compete effectively. That's not the case today and, while I personally find organized competition the most rewarding way to play paintball, it does have its issues and complications and may not be for everyone.

Despite my personal enthusiasm for tournament paintball, I have to be completely honest and say that competition paintball—both tournaments and scenario games—is *not* little league. If you show up at one of these events expecting it to be that organized and focused, you'll be terribly disappointed.

Competition paintball has not yet matured to the point where there is a national governing body, a standard set of rules, local organizations and all the other support networks and controls that go with organized youth sports.

This means that anyone, regardless of experience, integrity, ability or background, can call themselves a tournament promoter, organize an event or league, and start collecting fees (often extravagant fees) with little or no guarantee that they are going to deliver what they are promising to deliver.

Over the past several years, as the average player age has gotten lower and lower and more and more parents have been showing up at events, the following phrase has become all too common: "If *this* is what tournaments are all about, you're never going to another one again!"

Sad but true, especially when you consider how much better things could easily be. But all of that is probably a subject for another book...

This reaction to tournament ball on parents' part is due to two factors—the first being their own expectations of what they are familiar with from other youth sports, the second being the inferior quality of many of these events.

Parents expect that youth sports will, for the most part, be run fairly. They expect that they'll be "youth" oriented events. They expect that if rules are found in the rule booklet, the same will be enforced on the field of play.

Paintball competitions are not, however, youth sports. They are events where paintball competition takes place, and just about anyone is allowed to compete. There are *young guns*—16 and under, high school and college-only competitions, but most of these are few and far between, and even at this level, a certain degree of unfairness or unprofessionalism can creep in.

The professionalism and quality of paintball competitions is almost directly related to the scope of such events; national level events are usually well run, while local events are, more often than not, poorly managed affairs.

Unfortunately, players get their start at the local level, so no matter what you do, if you want to be involved with the competition end of things, you're going to have to learn how to handle local tournaments...

Unless, of course, the competition route you take is the scenario game.

Scenario games (now referred to as *woodsball* by many) are

not strictly tournaments in the sense of a sporting competition. In essence, scenario games combine large-scale teams, paintball competition, role-playing, and more paintball.

These types of games usually last between 12 and 24 hours (24 being the most common), involve teams of 50 or more and a very large playing area that usually has: multiple buildings, forts, entrenchments, lots of props designed to enhance role-playing, and a *theme*—such as the invasion of space aliens, the CIA versus the drug cartel, *Monty Python's Holy Grail*—just about any subject imaginable and usually drawn from popular culture.

There is competition in the sense that points are awarded for various actions (such as holding a fort, capturing a specific prop), which are tallied up at the end of the game to declare a winner—but the emphasis is on having fun and role-playing. Some folks are given special *roles* to play and they go at it with tremendous gusto—trading props for game money, assassinating a leader with a poisoned soda can…

Scenario gamers form teams just like tournament players and they usually take themselves pretty seriously, competing for honors such as best team, sportsmanship award, etc., but they're not the rabidly competitive folks that you see at regular tournaments.

Scenario games offer an easier environment for an individual or small group to break into—just sign up and pay, and you'll be assigned to a team—and the commitment and time required is not nearly as intense as that experienced by players who are on a serious tournament team.

Perhaps the best way to describe the difference is that scenario gamers like good, clean, fun with a bit of competition thrown in, while tournament players are all about the competition and, if they happen to have fun along the way, it's a bonus. Scenario gamers are the bar league softball players of the industry; tournament players are the Little League MLB wannabes of the future.

Preparation for the scenario gamer is generally easier and less expensive than it is for the tournament player; there's no cultural requirement for a high-end gun, and no standard uniform (unless you count camouflage, which is pretty much de rigueur); at most games you can even rent your gear and play.

I'd suggest that the first time player simply play; get assigned to a squad, find out what the mission is and play your hardest. Watch, listen, and learn—hang out at the campsites (overnight affairs with the games usually starting at noon and ending at noon the following day, including a no-play break during the late-evening/early-morning. Most game providers have camping facilities on or near the event; sometimes the best part of these games is what happens off the field around the campfires). Ask questions and maybe find a local group can be hooked up with for future games.

Later on, once the lay of the land has been learned, the player can get more ambitious and play a role, join a team, and experience these games to their fullest extent.

A very recent development is a hybrid of scenarios and tournaments—often referred to as *woodsball* or *scenario* leagues. These are in many respects a return to the old-style of competition in the woods (as opposed to the open, inflatable fields) with multiple, scenario-style objectives to be gained during the course of the game. You can expect to see a mix of tournament and scenario sensibilities at events featuring this style of play.

As was said earlier, if your child is looking for true competition—team sports, the reward of victory, the agony of defeat, an organized environment, and all the things that go along with playing a team sport, competition or tournament paintball is the way to go. Unfortunately, there's no national organization to contact that can put you in touch with teams seeking players. No "Paintball Little League" exists—although it ought to.

There are really only two ways to get involved—join an existing team or start one of your own. The former is easier to do and less expensive, while the latter will give you greater control—and a lot of hard work. You (and your child, of course) are going to have to figure it out for yourselves, so I'd recommend finding a local team—preferably one that has other players your child's age already participating (although a few years in either direction makes little difference on a team; you either have game or you don't as far as the team is concerned.)

Your child will probably have to participate in a try-out or probationary period while the team leaders evaluate his or her play. If you're at this stage of the game—have your kid do all the work. You'll find out very quickly if your future paintball star really wants to do this. I suggest they find out the following beforehand:

- What kind of gear players are expected to have
- What skills are being looked for by the team
- What *positions* they are looking to fill
- What the player's commitment is expected to be
- Number of days of practice
- Number of events
- Amount of travel required
- *Fees*
- What benefits/sponsorship the team provides
- How, where, and when they go about trying out or joining

You can then discuss it, evaluate the costs (i.e., if practice fees are $50 a weekend for paint, entry and air, you're looking at approximately $2000 for the season) and the commitments (The more a player gets to practice and play with a focused team, the better their game will become.). Then decide if this might be the team for you (I mean, your child).

If there were any possibility that you and the paintball star might be putting your own team together in the future, I'd make myself a part of the practices and events. Compare the kind of training your child is receiving from the paintball team to the training they'd get from an intramural sports team. If it seems sub-par, it probably is (since formal training regimens are really just beginning to take hold in paintball), and you might want to look elsewhere—or hop in with some suggestions to your kid. Make sure to learn as much as you can about organizing and operating a team (so long as the people doing the job seem to have a clue) before you make that jump to your own.

The only reason to join a team, other than the competition, is to gain support and sponsorship for what is admittedly a relatively expensive sport.

When most people think of sponsorship, they think of a corporate entity footing the bill. "Phil's Bail Bonds" paid for the uniforms... "McGregor's Supermarket" for the bats and balls. You probably won't be surprised if I say that it's not like that in paintball.

From reading the magazines and watching the videos, most up-and-coming tournament players get it into their heads that someday, in the not-too-distant future, some wonderful people from the paintball industry are going to pay for the gun, the mask, the clothing, the tank, the travel, the uniform and the paintballs. They'll be able to play every day of the week for free, their picture will be splashed on the covers of all the magazines, and somehow there's going to be a roof over their head, food in the fridge and a gassed-up car in the garage...

Sorry to paint this false and misleading picture of paintball sponsorship, but darned if it isn't the most popular and persistent one.

Sponsorship takes many forms in the paintball industry. There are a few (very, very few) players at the top of the game who are making a decent living playing paintball—*as long as they do well at the paintball company they also happen to work for.*

Most sponsorship takes the form of support. Rather than having to pay full retail for your gear, you'll pay a wholesale cost. Rather than paying for all of your paint, you'll get some every week or every month at a reduced price. Instead of having to pay the entire entry fee, a portion of it is subsidized.

Make no mistake; in a game where the average player's annual budget is 7.5 to 10 thousand dollars per year, shaving anything off is a big help. (And if you think about it, your two primary expenses are paintballs and travel, so any help in those areas will go a long way towards reducing that budget.) The message here is that even if your child is a paintball star, they'll still not be playing for free.

A Note On Sponsorships

Since there are no formal regulations or organizations governing who can play for whom, players and teams are subject to being *cherry-picked*—lured away from their current team by offers of better sponsorship.

I would caution a wise parent to examine why their child is playing paintball when it comes to making decisions on who they play for.

While having playing expenses covered is a tremendous boon, the real question becomes: why have they offered my child this support? Maybe your child is a star player (or will develop into one under the correct tutelage); or it just may be a political move, even an economic move. The team seeking out your child could actually be looking to: gut the team currently played for, influence the local market by getting your child to use certain gear, or find and milk a cash cow.

I would *always* question the motives of anyone making a sponsorship offer to your child. You and your child need to find out if the offer is a real and lasting one—or just a temporary one. *Who* will your kid be playing with? What's their track record? Is the sponsorship offer real or just a carrot? What guarantees are being offered? What happens to your child's current team?

A Note On Other Team-Related Issues

There's so much to learn and figure out when it comes to teams that I can't really do justice to all of the issues within the pages of this book. If you can scare up a copy of my old *Maxing: A Guide to Winning Tournament Play*, it's a good start; otherwise, jump in and watch everything with an eagle eye and a good dose of common sense. If you can't get my book, here are some other pointers:

Prizes & Prize Money: There are as many ways of handling the winnings as there are teams, but in most cases, this issue is resolved in a couple of common ways. It is not unusual for the team sponsor or owner to retain the prizes won at events for re-sale. They're laying out the bucks and are entitled. It's also not uncommon for the prizes to be split equally if players are footing the bill. (I suggest the following in this case: put a price tag on the gear, allow players on the team to take first pick at that price, sell any remaining gear and split the cash amongst the players who didn't take the gear. If there isn't enough gear to go around, sell it all and split the cash.) Above all, put a prize policy in place *before* you win anything. It's also not unusual for a team to sell prizes back to an event for cash (usually well below its street value), nor is it unknown to hook the team up with a store or field that purchases all winnings for a set percentage of the product's MSRP.

Regardless of the policy, don't count on covering the play and practice fees with prize winnings—even the top teams barely break even on a season.

Politics, Benching, Psychology, etc: Some teams base their roster picks on skill. Most base their picks on friendships, or on political influence ("Dad is the team's primary sponsor."); still others probably consult the mystics of the East for all the sense they display in how they go about determining who will play and who will not—especially at major events. Teams also go through gyrations trying to determine: who is going to play how many games at an event, whether players who play fewer games pay the same fee, whether substitutes pay at all unless they play, etc.

Have your child ask what these rules for the team are. A serious team plays their best squad and brings a couple of players as substitutes. Well-sponsored teams don't worry about the cost of a game. It's not unusual, though, for a substitute who rides the bench all event long to also have to pay part of the entry fee. There are no hard and fast rules. Some teams *rotate*, attempting to give each player attending an event an equal, or close to equal number of games; others will play subs when they have a *lock* on advancing to the next round or when the game's outcome doesn't matter. The guiding principal should not be how much a player spends, but is the selection done in a reasonably fair, sensible manner? If your child is being taken advantage of (always going to an event, always paying to do so, and never getting a game in), encourage them to find another team or to agitate for some change.

Team Deals: Quite often, a team is really just an excuse for a field or storeowner who wants to make a steady income. This is usually identifiable when the team spends all kinds of money but doesn't really improve with time, or doesn't go anywhere, or if the cash cows on the team never end up on the event roster. The same is true for farm teams; often the second, third and fourth level teams associated with a field are really there to support the main team monetarily, as well as to serve as a source of fresh talent.

Provided that you can help your paintball playing progeny find a well-run team and avoid the previously mentioned pitfalls, tournament play can confer all of the benefits your child would obtain from playing any other organized sport.

CHAPTER 9:
LOCAL SUPPORT ORGANIZATIONS

ORGANIZED YOUTH PLAY

In 1999 the paintball industry made several key moves that opened the game up to younger players. Product pricing came way down and schools, churches, youth service organizations, PAL and other such groups began to embrace the game as a way to provide healthy exercise to young players. The Boy Scouts of America and Scouting USA continue to maintain a ban on playing paintball as an officially endorsed activity, even though it would seem to be a natural for them. We've never gotten a really clear explanation, but we do know that Troops regularly play in a non-official capacity.

This kind of play is still in its grass roots stages, with little or no national level organization. However, this does present opportunities for the enterprising paintballer. Most stores and fields are willing to offer discounts to groups—especially if they are well organized and can offer a decently-sized group that will purchase and play regularly.

Around about 1998 several college students banded together and formed independent college-based leagues, restricting play to players attending the schools in the league. This led to the first-ever National College Championship (hosted by the author) and the eventual creation of the *National College Paintball Association*, which hosts multiple events annually, as well as providing an umbrella for regional associations to operate under. High school-level play is also beginning to start up, working with the NCPA and hosting at least one national level event for high school-aged children.

Although not embraced by the likes of the NCAA, College Level paintball is making some headway (recently signing a deal with a cable broadcaster) and helping to reduce the costs for college students who wish to compete.

Churches are also becoming more and more organized, most around Youth Pastor ministries—paintball is apparently an attention-getter! One such organization serving this need is the *Christian Paintball Players Association* (CPPA). These groups tend to mix ministry, paintball, moral values, and worship into their efforts, and if you and your family are so inclined, they offer an excellent opportunity to participate in the sport at many different levels. Some have even gone so far as to organize play on Saturdays so that the kids can get their tournament in and still attend services on Sunday.

While still in its nascent years, nationally-organized youth paintball play is growing in popularity and will probably become a major focus of the industry over the next few years. Getting your child involved now is probably a good idea, as growth leads to opportunity.

SCHOOLS AND PAINTBALL

Most public high schools these days have at least a core group of players, if not a full-blown paintball club. If your child's school does have one, all the better. They'll find some ready teammates and will probably benefit from discounts at playing fields and retail stores that support the club.

If not, this might be a good time for your child to learn all about civic activity.

The rules and regulations for extra-curricular activities vary from school to school, but most are usually looking for the following:

- Some support from the community—a mentor, a group of parents requesting it,
- A reputable local field/or store willing to work with the club,

- Students who are vocal supporters of the concept (the more, the better),
- Parents who are articulate, respectable and who can address concerns knowledgably,
- A teacher or staff member willing to be the school's representative,
- Persistence.

Most schools require something like the following when considering a club activity:
- Is it a safe, community-accepted activity?
- Are they (positively) familiar with it—even in passing?
- Are the safety issues well covered?
- What is the school's liability likely to be?

More often than not, with enough students signing a petition and a carefully written proposal, a school will accept the idea of a paintball club on a probationary status. (This usually means it will be an official school club, but will not yet receive funding from the school).

If I were trying to get a club going at one of our local high schools, I'd do the following:
- Get a rough idea of how many students already play, even if only part time,
- Find a staff member to partner with,
- Find out the requirements for getting a club started,
- Find a local field willing to give students from the club a discounted rate,
- Find a local store willing to give students from the club a discounted rate,
- Have my child conduct a preliminary survey with a petition requiring other students to sign up,
- Write up (with my child) the proposal to the

school, including the number of interested students, the community support already obtained, a copy of the field waiver (to show responsibility and liability coverage by the field) and *strong* endorsement of whatever rules, regulations and requirements the school may have (such as, no paintballs, paintball guns or paintball gear on school campus).

After that, it's up to the school administration, the local school board, and any concerned parents there might be. You'll need to stress that *parental permission* for participation is required; you'll probably need to make provisions for students who can't afford their own gear; and you'll probably have to play a little politics on the local level. Don't get antagonistic or combative, and remember that you don't have to have the school's blessing to form a club for high school students.

If your child is in grade school or junior high, you'll be running into age restriction issues (since paintball insurance only covers ages 10 and older), so I'd wait until high school. If your child is college bound, put them in touch with the NCPA (National College Paintball Association)—chances are there's already a team at the school they'll be attending.

CHAPTER 10:
PAINTBALL AS MOTIVATOR

USING PAINTBALL AS AN INCENTIVE

Since time immemorial, parents have sought ways to encourage, entice, interest, bribe and force their children to behave in the desired manner, apply themselves to work and study, strive to better themselves, embrace the same values that their parents believe in, and to generally do for themselves what needs to be done in order to live a healthy, happy and successful life. In other words, get them out of the house with the wherewithal to be able to fend for themselves.

While there are numerous schools of thought on the proper way to go about doing this (and we won't endorse any particular form of child-rearing here), a few hard and fast rules apply to them all.

First, being involved directly with your child and their activities. Everyone laments the good old days of the stay-at-home mom (or dad, a relatively recent innovation)—not because they want to return to the politically incorrect days of male chauvinism, but because it provided children with at least one parent who was immediately on hand to reinforce lessons and values.

Today, it's more difficult than ever; chances are the kid's daily schedule is even more hectic than the parents'. Nevertheless, a little interest and encouragement by a parent goes a long way towards keeping a child focused. The more involved you are, the earlier you will be able to spot issues and problems, and the faster you'll be able to offer correction and guidance.

Since I have no clue what your family dynamic is, I can't really offer a specific way to achieve greater and more meaningful involvement in your child's life. I can reiterate others who have said that watching grades from school and spending regularly scheduled time every day with your child are a minimal requirement.

I'll also suggest that time spent with the children should include both the things you are interested in and the things *they* are interested in. Questions about schoolwork can be followed by questions about paintball. When you demonstrate interest in the things important to your children, it reinforces the importance of the other things you express an interest in, whether they are equally important to your child or not.

Second, having a goal helps maintain focus, can confer a sense of accomplishment and, perhaps most importantly of all, helps parent's keep track of progress. The goal might be improving grades in a particular subject. *How* that is accomplished is up to you. Discussing the desired result with your child and then stating the goal is the most important step.

Paintball provides an opportunity for both involvement AND goal setting. The things your child has to do on the paintball field are exactly the same things they have to do in order to be successful in anything else in life.

In order to play in a game of paintball, your child needs to learn new information and new skills, they need to understand objectives and goals, they have to learn how to apply their new knowledge to achieving those objectives and goals, and they will see the immediate results of their actions and choices.

In order to learn a subject in school, your child will obtain new information, their goal will be to demonstrate a mastery of that new knowledge, they'll take tests where they will apply that new knowledge, and their grades will show the consequences of their choices.

I've seen paintball-playing privileges being used by parents in a number of effective ways that break down into the two classics of motivation—honey and vinegar.

On the vinegar side, we have: suspension of playing privileges, withdrawal of playing budget, the confiscation of paintball equipment.

On the honey side, we have: contribution/subsidy of playing budget for maintaining/improving grades, purchase of a major piece of equipment as a reward for achieving grade goals, playing privileges contingent upon maintenance of grades.

This extends to household chores, visiting unpopular relatives, successful participation in other desired, non-school activities, and general behavior, "If you don't stop teasing your sister, you can forget about playing this weekend."

Regardless of what mix you employ, it's important to have a hard and fast set of rules and to stick by them: consistency is often more important than fairness. Depending upon your child's level of involvement, you may need to plan ahead a little bit and weigh the consequences of your own actions. For example, if your child is a starting player on a successful team that will be playing for the national championship next month, the suspension of playing privileges for a valid reason is a much stronger punishment than not being able to play during a regular weekend practice. Your decision will also be affecting a number of other individuals (the rest of the team), and you might be dealing with pressure from them to relent from your decision.

If you've set the rules and stuck by them, no one from outside your family has any right to question or interfere with your decisions, but you do need to be mindful that in a team setting, your decisions can end up punishing other people.

Above all, I'd implement the rules I've established for kids playing on the teams that I personally work with:

- Parents and their rules come first.
- Schoolwork, chores and family responsibilities come

before the team.

Most successful paintball incentive programs I'm familiar with contain the following elements:

1. A grade point average performance level is established: for example, the student must maintain a B+ throughout the school year.

2. All extracurricular activities deemed more important than paintball must be properly engaged in (i.e., practices for the school marching band are not missed)

3. A set of prohibited behaviors are established (no reports for unruly behavior, no talking back to mom).

4. A set of routine chores are established (keeping the room clean, taking out the garbage, cutting the lawn).

5. A method for earning money is created (an allowance, a part-time after-school job, payment for chores that are not routine...).

Successful completion of the above is discussed with the child so that the parents' expectations—and the "rules of engagement" are clearly delineated. Disagreement, confusion or a misunderstanding of expectations are an impediment to success, so now is the time to identify such things and straighten them out.

The consequences of failing to meet those expectations are clear; if the grade point average drops, no play until they're brought back up again. If the lawn isn't cut come Saturday morning—no play.

The incentives can then be brought in to encourage the child to go beyond what is normally expected. For example, if you believe that math is your child's most important subject, you can offer to purchase them a desired piece of equipment if they achieve an A in that subject—half a grade point beyond your minimal B+ requirement. Or, if your child needs to earn more money for play, you can offer to pay them a few dollars for doing the hedge trimming—in addition to cutting the lawn.

Be mindful that the goals you set are easier to monitor and to achieve if they are shorter-term and specific. Improvement in a grade on a particular test this week, instead of improvement in the subject by the end of the marking period; better behavior displayed toward a sibling for the next two days—instead of for life…

The age of your child also has a lot to do with what your incentive strategy is going to be; if they are under 15, chances are that their only source of income is going to be the parents, be it the traditional allowance or the ages -old begging-and-pleading, or, my personal favorite—saving up birthday and holiday money. (Second only to skipping lunch in school so they can pocket the lunch money…). When the child can have no independent source of income, it's even more important to have the rules set for what they must do before they can spend *your* money. In order to help them prepare for a future job, it's probably a good idea to give them some tasks they can do to earn a little. This will also give you an opportunity to teach them all about saving, how to budget ("If you buy candy now, you won't have enough left to play paintball this weekend,"), and the proper ways to handle money.

Children 15 to 16 and older are pretty much expected to get a job—delivering papers, yard work, flipping burgers. At this age they've begun to experience and demand a little more independence and are expected to be taking their work responsibilities seriously, which means that they are also expected to be budgeting their earnings. It might be a good idea at this point to sit down and help your child analyze their budget needs and address the inevitable shortfalls. How much are they bringing in each week (allowance, wages) and what do they need to spend it on? A lesson in disposable versus nondisposable income is appropriate at this point. What do they need to be saving for (prom night, the car they'll be purchasing in a few years) and how much of their weekly income is going towards savings?

What little is left over is for fun, and undoubtedly will not be as much as they'd like it to be. Now you have an opportunity to discuss ways and means of closing the gap, such as whether they can get an hour or two extra out of their job. Is there some way to reduce spending on other necessities (bringing a bag lunch to school instead of buying it in the cafeteria)? Maybe they could even get a job at the local paintball field.

The bottom line is this: paintball is an activity that most children are extremely motivated to participate in, and you can use their own desire and interest to help you instill the values and behaviors you desire.

CHAPTER 11:
PARENTS SHOULD HAVE SOME FUN TOO

GETTING INTO THE GAME YOURSELF

Hopefully, after reading through this entire self-help guide, learning that paintball is a healthy, safe and fun activity, you'll have a bit of a hankering to play yourself. This I strongly encourage, as paintball is a perfectly fine activity for families to enjoy together. There's even been a tournament team (The Family) that did quite well for a few years on the circuit, all of whose members were father, mother, son, daughter and cousins.

I'd be just a little wary of cramping your child's style. You might think it's a great idea for getting together with the kids, while your child may want to use paintball as time away from the family. Otherwise, I can think of no other valid reason that parents and siblings shouldn't join in the fun.

Just remember, if you do start playing, the family paintball budget is going to approach the astronomical; on the other hand, if there's some talent in the family, you just might be able to line up some sponsorship and hit the road together.

CHAPTER 12:
PAINTBALL AS A BUSINESS

GETTING INTO THE BUSINESS

There has been, of late, an alarming trend on the part of paintball parents. They look at how much money they and their kids spend on the game, they look at how popular the game is, and two weeks later they've opened up a field or store, shaving expenses by getting their kid's gear at dealer pricing and trying to make a living in the paintball industry.

I probably shouldn't have to say this, but your child's hobby is probably not a good excuse for opening a business.

Paintball remains a niche or specialty market, and there is still a very strong good-old-boy network (guys like myself who have been in it from the beginning). That translates into a lot of specialty knowledge, which takes years to acquire; there are political and relationship issues that those new to the sport are unfamiliar with and which can have a tremendous impact on a business.

The specialty knowledge (what product to purchase, how to analyze the local market, how to sell, identifying trends) is true for any business, but there is a difference in paintball. When you pull up to a McDonalds and order a quarter-pounder with cheese, what you get is a quarter-pounder with cheese, regardless of whether the franchise owner was Hamburger U's very first *summa cum laude* graduate or the ink is still wet on the franchise check . When you go into a paintball store or step onto a playing field, the experience is vastly different depending on whether the owner/operator has been in business for years or just finished inflating the last bunker.

Paintball is *very* trend-conscious, very immediate, very

161

word-of-mouth. People who know the game are readily apparent. Posers are almost immediately spotted. Therefore, with rare exception, the neophyte store/field owner is going to be viewed by consumers who have influence as a newbie. The mistaken use of terminology, the stocking of crappy gear, the endorsement of a product line, event or personality that runs counter to the culture, will immediately brand you as that worst of all paintball characters, a know-nothing wanna-be playa or worse, "the idiot who just got into the game and has the gall to think he's good enough to start selling gear, is only doing it to save himself a few bucks, so why aren't I getting the same break?"

In short, there's a very strong pay-your-dues streak inherent in the industry, and this is where the politics and personalities enter into the equation from the outside—you'd never guess that if you stock product A, Company B will not sell to you. It's even less likely you'll find out that a particular set of teams won't frequent your store or field because the field or store owner down the road told them not to...

All of that before we even get to the straight business considerations. So, the first thing I would caution is—treat it like you would any other serious business venture. Do not expect to make a profit without having to invest time, energy and hard work. It may look easy, but it's just as hard—if not harder—to make a go of a paintball business as in any other business.

The next thing to do is to examine your market. Maybe you're lucky and just happen to live in a region where paintball is underdeveloped (*very* unlikely). If that's the case, you'll really need to dig to identify the *underground paintball market*—the people running renegade fields, the people selling out of the garage for 10% over cost, the players who have good hook-ups or who sell tournament winnings or product received as partial sponsorship.

If there appears to be a lack of competition, or if the existing businesses are deficient in some area, there just may be a chance for you to make a go of it.

Next, figure out whether you're going to do a store or a field. You really ought to do both because the synergy of a field feeding a store and a store feeding a field has become the standard way to operate. You need the field so that your store customers have somewhere to play and you need the store so that your field customers have somewhere to buy their gear.

Now comes the big hurdle—finding a location and obtaining the hardware and products.

Location is everything; cheap land is usually surrounded by cheap people—which means a local base that probably can't afford to play. Too high a cost for rent/lease, and your overhead will kill you.

The investment in product and hardware to run your games is going to shock you. Basic inventory for a store—guns, tanks, loaders, clothing, paint, accessories, magazines, cleaning supplies will swallow up 30 to 50 thousand dollars and leave you wondering what you're going to put on the shelves. High-end markers will cost a dealer close to one thousand a pop, for which the dealer can expect to clear maybe 200 dollars. Here's just one example: playing pants. Your chosen manufacturer sells these to you at $75 per pair. There are four color schemes, and sizes ranging from 30 to 44. Laying in one pair of each size in each color will run you about $2500...just for pants.

If your chosen paintball business is a playing site, get set for the fun. Chances are you'll spend more money on attorneys, dealing with local ordnances, zoning boards and county councils, than you will on equipment. You'll need several acres of land with year-round access, you'll have to clear the land and probably grade it as well, and then you'll have to lay in a few sets of bunkers that last maybe two seasons of hard use and cost anywhere from $1800 to $7500 each.

163

There's more to learn when operating a field than there is to running a retail store. You'll have fun dealing with weather issues, neighbor issues, liability issues, and so much more.

The industry politics, though, are usually the bugaboo—people you don't know interfering with your business for reasons you are totally unaware of (such as their friend owning a field in the next town over).

If you do decide to go into business—find trustworthy people in the industry, dot all of your I's and cross all of your T's, cross your fingers and hope for the best. And, by the way, welcome to the industry!

GLOSSARY OF PAINTBALL TERMS

300 FPS: The upper legal velocity of a paintball at commercial sites and paintball events.

".68" refers to the most common caliber of paintball.

After Market: A sometimes pejorative term used to describe upgrades and/or parts not made by the original manufacturer.

Agitator: Specifically, the component in an electronic loader that jostles the paintballs (such as a paddle)— sometimes used to refer to an entire electronic loader.

Airball: An open playing field where all of the bunkers are inflatables.
   A game of paintball played on a field with inflatable bunkers.
   The act of firing without a paintball being discharged during a game.

Airsmith: A paintball marker technician (also known as a Gun Tech).

Anti-Doubler: A device for preventing more than one paintball from loading into the breech at a time—usually a flexible device that protrudes into the breech and which can be pushed out of the way by the bolt.

Anti-Siphon (tube): A device for preventing liquid CO_2 from being drawn out of a tank.

Arm Band: A piece of colored material used to designate team assignment -- conventionally worn on the upper left arm.

ASA: Acronym for Air Source Adapter, a device for converting a standard bottle thread to a more common thread, such as 1/8 NPT—bottomlines, expansion chambers and On/Off tank adapters are different versions of ASA's.

B

Ball Break: A ball that breaks in an inconvenient location, such as inside a tube, loader, barrel or breech.

Ball Detent: One of several different types of anti-doubler device.

Barrel Break: A paintball that shatters inside a gun's barrel instead of exiting.

Barrel Condom: A sleeve fitted over a gun barrel to prevent accidental discharge.

Barrel Plug: A safety device fitted into a gun barrel that prevents accidental discharge.

Barrel Tap (rule): Game rule variation that allows a player to "tag" or "tap" a bunker with a gun barrel to eliminate an opponent instead of shooting then from close range.

BBD: Acronym for Barrel Blocking Device. This acronym was created to cover both barrel "condoms" and barrel "plugs."

Big Game: A format in which the objective is to have as many players per team as possible—which has metamorphosed into the scenario game, although there are still several annual big game events

Bolt: A primary component of paintball guns—in most gun designs, the bolt is used to push the paintball into the barrel and vent gas down the barrel to fire the ball.

Blind Fire: The act of shooting a gun without looking to see where it is aimed or where the shots are hitting –
an illegal action at most commercial paintball fields.

Blow Back (semi-auto): A generally inexpensive style of paintball gun design which utilizes excess gas to re-cock the mechanism.

Blow Back: Gas leaking around the bolt of a paintball gun due to improper sealing of the mechanism.

Bonus Ball: Shooting an eliminated player again, once they are leaving the field.

Bottle: A common name for an air tank.

Bottom Line: Originally a trade name for a specific style of ASA, it has now come to refer to virtually any device which has a bottle thread adapter and is attached to the bottom of a grip frame.

Bounce 1: A ball failing to break on impact—99% of the time, a "bounce" does not count for an elimination.

Bounce 2 (Bouncing): The electronic noise created by an

electronic switch; using the 'noise' to cause a paintball gun to fire—usually multiple times per trigger pull.

Bouncer: A ball that fails to break on impact.

BPS: Acronym for Balls-Per-Second, a unit of measure used to indicate how fast a paintball gun can fire.

Break (Break out, On The Break, The Break): The start of a competition, short for "Breakout" (players breaking out of their starting location).

Bunker: A man-made obstacle used to provide cover and protection during a paintball game, most bunkers being of the inflatable variety—to 'Bunker' someone means to run up and shoot them from a very close distance (usually inches) and is common in tournament play. (Other terms: Bunkering, Bunkered).

Burst Disc: A pressure relief device built into all paintball gas tanks.

BYOP: An acronym for Bring Your Own Paint, which is used to indicate that players are allowed to use paintballs not purchased at a facility or event

C

Caliber: A unit of measure borrowed from firearms technology, usually expressed as a percentage of an inch The most common caliber used in paintball is .68, or 68/100ths of an inch.

CGA: Acronym for the Compressed Gas Association.

Check Valve: A self-closing valve or a valve which only allows flow in a single direction, used on the filling port of a high-pressure tank.

Cheese: An inflatable bunker resembling a cheese or pizza wedge.

Chop (chopped): A ball break in a gun's breech, usually caused by failure of the ball to load properly, where the ball is "chopped" in half by the action of the gun's bolt—usually the worst kind of ball break in a gun.

Chrono, Chronograph: A device used to measure the velocity of a paintball; the act of testing the velocity of a paintball gun.

Clean: A referee's call, used to indicate that a player who was suspected of having a hit on them was not hit.

CO_2: A common gas, comprised of oxygen and carbon, currently the propellant most often used in the game of paintball.

Compressed Air: High-pressure air used for a propellant in paintball guns (synonymous with HPA and Nitrogen).

Concept Field: Another name for a playing field consisting of inflatable bunkers.

Condom: Shortened form of Barrel Condom.

Constant Air: Originally a trade name, this term became synonymous with using a large, tank-based gas supply, as opposed to disposable cartridges.

Count (the): This tournament term refers to the current number of live players remaining on the field during a game. Teams employ code words to keep track of how many opponents have been eliminated and how many of their teammates have been eliminated. Asking "what's the count" means the player wants to know the total of all eliminations and losses. "Losing" the count means that a team has a mistaken idea of how many opponents are left on the field.

Cycle (rate): Usually interchangeable with Rate-of-Fire or Balls-per-Second as a unit of measure of a gun's operating speed—proper usage refers to the theoretical upper limit of a marker's mechanical operation.

D

Dead Box: A contained area on a field where eliminated players go until the current game ends.

Detent: Slang for "anti-doubler."

Direct Feed: One of several older methods of introducing a paintball from the loader into the breech, this usually denotes a tube mounted at 45 degrees to the body of the marker.

Dorito: An inflatable bunker resembling a Dorito™ chip in profile.

E

Elbow: Originally an angled adapter for attaching a loader to a direct feed tube on the gun, it now refers to any adapter, regardless of shape, for attaching a loader to a marker.

Expansion Chamber: A volumizing device, most commonly used with CO_2—the large volume area inside allows liquid CO_2 a better chance to turn into gas before reaching the gun's valve.

F

Feeder: An alternate name for a loader.

Fifty (the): The center of a tournament paintball field, represented by a line running the width of the field, or the central portion of the field set off with a different color.

Fill Port: A standard adapter which allows high pressure tanks to be connected to a fill station.

Fill Station: The equipment used to fill either CO_2 or high-pressure air tanks and/or the location at a playing field where a player obtains tank fills.

Flag Station: A marked off area on a playing field that the game flag is either placed in and/or the location a flag must be brought to in order to win the game.

Flash: The process of uploading new programming to an electronic paintball marker.

Foregrip: A device, usually attached to the forward part of a marker, that the player can hold for additional shooting stability.

FPS: Acronym for Feet-Per-Second, used to refer to the velocity of a paintball when it exits the barrel.

Full Auto (Fully Automatic): A firing mode which allows the marker to continuously fire as long as the trigger is depressed.

G

Gas Efficiency: Usually refers to how much/little pressurized gas is used to operate a marker and fire a paintball.

Gogged: Getting shot in the goggles (usually referring to the humiliation associated with such a shot).

Going Liquid: Liquid CO_2 enters the valve chamber and raises the velocity of the marker.

Grip, Grip Frame: The trigger frame portion of a paintball gun.

Guppy: An archaic term for a loader or pod, originally a trade name.

H

Harness: Archaic term for a butt pack—load-bearing gear was originally a chest harness.

Hickey, sucker mark, red tattoo: The welt caused by a paintball impact.

Hit: A paintball breaking on a player.

Home Base: An inflatable bunker that resembles a home base in profile (a pentagonal bunker).

Hopper: Most commonly refers to a loader, this is also used to refer to a feed system.

Hoser: A player who indiscriminately fires their marker.

Hosing: The act of firing large volumes of paint.

Hosed (get hosed, got hosed, getting hosed): A player who was eliminated either by a large number of hits, or a player eliminated in a spectacular fashion.

Hot (shooting hot): A marker that is firing over the legal velocity limit; a marker that shot over the limit due to a malfunction or improper set-up.

HPA: Acronym for High Pressure Air, this is generally used to refer to a pressure tank used with a paintball gun. Synonymous with Compressed Air and Nitrogen.

Hydro, Hydro Date, Hydrostatic Test: Refers to the act or requirement of obtaining a pressure test for high- pressure tanks.

I

Inflatable: A large vinyl shape used as a bunker on a paintball field.

J

Jimmy: A trade name utilizing a slang term for condom and designating a Barrel Condom.

K

Kill: The elimination of an opponent.

Kill Count: The total number of opponents eliminated.

Kill Code: A code word used by a team to announce eliminations of opponents and losses of teammates during a game.

Knuckle: A portion of a snake bunker that protrudes from the bunker.

L

Laning: The act of firing down an alley on a field to keep opponents from moving.

Laydown: A low bunker (usually cylindrical) that only provides protection if players are lying down behind it.

Lit Up, Lite Up: A player who received multiple hits while being eliminated.

Loader: A magazine device for a paintball gun.

Longball: The act of shooting (accurately) at extreme ranges.

LPR, Low Pressure Regulator: Used in paintball guns to lower the input pressure of gasses that operate internal mechanisms.

M

Marker: Politically-correct name for a paintball gun.

Muzzle Velocity: The speed at which a paintball is traveling immediately upon exiting the barrel.

N

Nitrogen, Nitro, N_2: A naturally occurring gas that when compressed is used as a propellant for paintball guns—most 'nitrogen' is actually compressed air. (Synonymous with HPA and Compressed Air).

O

O-Ring: A pressure seal made out of an elastic material and commonly used on pressure tanks and internally in paintball markers/guns.

P

Paint Check: Originally a call used by players to gain the attention of a referee to check the legality of a hit.

Plug: Shortened form of Barrel Plug.

Pod: A paintball carrying device, also referred to as a tube or loader.

Ports: Small holes drilled down the length of a barrel, used to quiet the barrel; an air passage.

Poser: A player pretending to be a skilled player.

Push: A "charge" during a paintball game.

Q

Quick-Disconnect: One of several different kinds of fittings that allow pressure lines to be connected and disconnected easily.

R

Ramp, ramping: A paintball gun (electronic) that automatically increases either velocity, rate of fire or both, under program control, this is usually considered an illegal electronic cheating method.

Receiver: The main body of a paintball marker.

Remote Line, Remote, Remote System: An older method of connecting a pressure tank to a marker that uses a gas line, the tank is carried in a pouch on the back. Used to reduce weight of the marker, it is generally considered "old school."

Rifling: Grooves cut into the interior of a barrel, or holes drilled in the wall of a barrel in a (generally) spiral pattern, which presumably increases accuracy.

Rollie: A cylindrical inflatable bunker resting on its long axis.

S

Scenario Game: A format that lasts between 12 and 24 hours and incorporates elements of role playing and theme playing into the game.

Semi-Automatic (Semi-auto): A marker that re-cocks itself between shots so that it will fire every time the trigger is pulled.

Skirmish Line: Old-school term, now only applicable to scenario games; a line of players that stretches across the width of a field.

Slime, Slimed: Another word used to describe paint on a player or equipment.

Smacktalk: Caustic, abusive language, used on the field to rattle an opponent; used off the field to argue in an immature manner, but sometimes done in jest as the paintball form of "ranking" ("Yo Momma so fat...")

Snake: A long, low, series of bunkers, usually located along one side of a playing field and centered on the middle of the field.

Snatch Grip: A paintball gun grip with protrusions built into its lower portion that make it easier to grab and that support the hand.

Speedball: A paintball game played on a concept field—or a game played on a small field consisting of artificial terrain.

Splatter: The fill and shell that sprays away from a paintball when it breaks, this usually refers to paint that has landed on a player from a ricochet (not a direct hit).

Squeegee: A device for cleaning broken paint out of the barrel of a marker—generally interchangeable with "swab."

Staging Area: A marked-off area where players prepare for a game, this usually consists of cover, table and chairs, and is most often found at tournaments.

StandUp: A cylindrical inflatable bunker resting on its short access.

Swab: A device (usually wool) used to clean out barrels and pods.

Sweet Spotting: Firing at a designated location, instead of a target, this is a method used to catch players who will move through the area—also used to describe blind, but aimed fire. A player remains behind cover, but shoots at a designated location.

T

Tank: The container that holds pressurized gas used as a propellant for paintball guns.

Tape, Tape Line: The boundary around a playing field or the area of the field next to the boundary, the archaic term originated from the 'surveyors' tape' used to mark field boundaries in the woods.

Toasted: A player who was eliminated in a spectacular manner, this usually refers to a large number of hits on a single player.

Tombstone: An inflatable bunker resembling the top of a curved headstone.

Tournament: A formal competition between paintball teams.

Tournament Cap, Tourney Cap: A device mounted on either a marker or a tank to prevent the player from adjusting velocity during a game.

Tourneyball: Tournament and/or competition-oriented paintball play.

Three-Way: A pneumatic 'switching' device used on some paintball guns.

Tricked, (Tricked Out): Used to describe custom work, usually mill work and carving of a paintball gun body.

Trigger Job: Custom work done to a marker's trigger to make it easier and faster to pull.

Tunnel Vision: The 'mistake' of focusing on a single location or opponent during a game.

Twelve Gram: The original gas source for paintball; a small cylinder, holding 12 grams of CO_2 under pressure.

TWiB: Acronym for Tournament Wannabe, this indicates a player who talks the talk but doesn't walk the walk of a tournament player, or who acts unreasonably aggressive and justifies these action by stating that they are required for tournament play.

V

Valve: The device inside a marker allowing pressurized gas to flow from the source down the marker barrel.

Velocity Adjuster: Usually found at the rear of a marker, this device adjusts the marker's muzzle velocity.

Venturi (bolt): Refers to an arrangement of shaped or angled gas ports in the face of a gun bolt. It is believed by many that special configurations of gas ports can help increase accuracy, gas efficiency and/or range.

W

Walk On: A player not connected with a team who shows up at a field to play, or a recreational player.

Wannabe: A player with no skill who adopts the equipment, clothing and language of one who does.

Wipe, Wiping: The act of removing a valid hit during a paintball game in order to remain in the game.

Woodsball: A semi-derogatory term used to describe paintball play on natural terrain—usually referring to scenario games—which originally referred to any play in the woods.

APPENDIX A

BEFORE YOU PLAY: A checklist for a day of paintball play. By going down this list and marking off the boxes associated with a piece of gear or an activity, you'll be sure to have everything you need for a typical day of play.

PRELIMINARY PREPARATION

[ ] Directions to the playing site _____
_____

[ ] Games Played from _____until _____
[ ] Contact information for the playing site _____
_____

[ ] Transportation to the playing site arranged
[ ] Transportation from the playing site arranged
[ ] For Minors – Parental Consent form signed
[ ] Field Waiver completed
[ ] Entry fee, paint and air fees in hand
[ ] Medical issues reviewed and covered; any required medications in hand, proper authorities informed of pre-existing medical conditions

GEAR

[ ] Gear Bag   [ ] Mask
[ ] Marker   [ ] Loader
[ ] Harness   [ ] Tubes
[ ] Air Tank   [ ] Tools
[ ] Replacement & wear parts   [ ] Paintball appropriate clothing
[ ] Pants   [ ] Jersey
[ ] Gloves   [ ] Paintball appropriate footwear
[ ] Cleaning supplies   [ ] Padding
[ ] Knee pads   [ ] Elbow pads
[ ] Groin protection/breast protection
[ ] Neck protector
[ ] Hat or beanie   [ ] Additional/backup/extra gear
[ ] Car Keys   [ ] Wallet
[ ] Cell Phone   [ ] Drink
[ ] Snack food or a meal

APPENDIX B

INTERNET RESOURCES

News & Information Sites:

www.68caliber.com
A news and information resource, 68 Caliber usually breaks most of the industry news first. Generally good coverage of events.

www.About.Paintball.com
The paintball section at About.com. Good basic intro to the game and a variety of good links.

www.PBReview.com
The Internet's premiere independent product review site. Game participants are encouraged to submit product reviews. Beware though, that sometimes industry politics can greatly affect a product's rating.

www.P8ntballer.com
Europe's leading English language website.

www.WarPig.com
The industry's oldest and longest operating Internet portal.

Magazine & Publication Sites:

www.p8ntballer.com
The website for Paintball Games International magazine, a British publication with broad international coverage and a "cheeky" approach.

www.PaintballX3.com
A new site by the former editors of Paintball 2Xtremes, formerly one of the leading publications in the industry.

www.Splatmagazine.com
A relative newcomer, content may be too "racy" for some parents. Available at WalMart and other chain stores, this magazine is growing in popularity.

www.ActionPursuitGames.com
The industry's first nationally distributed monthly publication. (The author's first article appeared in this publication.)

Other Sites:

www.automagsonline.com
Originally the "owners group" for 68 Automag users, this site is generally more high-brow than its compadres.

www.BigEvilOnline.com
An up-and-coming forum with a respectful community.

www.McarterBrown.com
One of the most "intelligent" forums on the web.

www.Paintballforum.com
Relatively new forum/community site.

www.Paintballguns.net/forum
Another new forum.

www.paintballsportsmag.com
General event and product coverage.

Community Sites:
These are sites that offer forums, chat, polls, etc.

www.PBNation.com
Currently the "hot" site to be on. Contents can sometimes be racy. Often VERY political.

www.PBFreedom
Another forum.

APPENDIX C

PAINTBALL ORGANIZATIONS

Tournament Organizations

www.college-paintball.com
Home of the National College Paintball Association
Hosts College and High School Only events

www.pspevents.com
Paintball Sports Promotions League
Hosts 5 Player events across the country

www.cfoa.com
Carolina Field Operator's Association
Hosts 5 Player events on the East Coast

www.gpl05.com
Global Paintball League
An NPPL Affiliate in the North East

www.nxl.com
The National X-Ball League
Hosts Professional events across the country

www.paintball-guns.com/pmi-paintball-tournament.htm
PMI Pure Energy Series
5 Player Series in Florida

www.expseries.com
Hosts 7 Player events in the East

www.bppinc.net Bullseye Paintball Productions
Hosts events in Florida

www.coastalpaintball.com
Atlantic Coast Tournament Series
5 Player events in the East

www.adrenalineforcetournament.com
Events on the West Coast

www.cvpl.com
Central Virginia Paintball League
5 Player events in Virginia

Scenario Game Organizations:

www.blackcatpaintball.com

www.mppgames.com
Millennium Paintball Productions

www.nocerproductions.com
Produces humorous games usually based on comedy films

www.playsppl.com
Operates a scenario league

www.waynes-world.com/wd24event.html
Wayne Dollack 24 Hour Scenario Games
The "inventor" of scenario games

Other Organizations:

www.paintball-org.com
Minnesota Paintball Association

www.christianpaintball.com
The Christian Paintball Players Association

www.mspa.us
Mid-South Paintball Association

www.stockclasspaintball.com
supports playing with original equipment and rules

APPENDIX D

Resources:

www.prostarsports.com
Home of the Field Operator's Guide and other publications.

www.hatherleighpress.com
Publisher of the *Complete Guide to Paintball* book.

www.paintball-pti.com
Paintball Training Institute – classes for techs, field operators, referees and more.

www.paintball.org
Paintball Sports Trade Association.

APPENDIX E

Manufacturers & Suppliers:

Please note, no Internet-only retailers are listed here. This is a comprehensive list of manufacturers by type of product. Many will not sell directly to consumers, but each can supply contact information for their dealers. I make no recommendations or representations about any of the products manufactured by these companies. Please note also that paintball-on-the-internet changes constantly and some of these web addresses may have changed or are no longer active.

Suppliers are listed alphabetically by product category.

Air Systems:

Airgun Designs – www.airgun.com
Archon – www.archonpaintball.com
Crossfire – www.crossfireinc.com
Custom Products – www.customproducts.us
Draxxus – www.draxxus.com
Dye – www.dyeprecision.com
Evil – www.evil-paintball.com
Guerrilla Air – www.guerrillaair.com
Macdev – www.macdev.net
Pursuit Marketing Inc – www.pminetwork.com
Smartparts – www.smartparts.com
Wdp – www.wdp-paintball.com

Barrels:

32 Degrees – www.32ice.com

Aardvark – www.aardvarkdirect.com
Aci – www.airconcepts.com
Aim Paintball – www.aimpaintball.com
Allen Paintball – www.allenpaintball.com
Blackpoint Engineering – www.bp-usa.com
Bt Paintball – www.bentippmann.com
Check It Products – www.checkitproducts.com
Chipley Custom Machine – www.chipleymachine.com
Cmi – www.paintballcmi.com
Component Concepts – www.phantomonline.com
Crossfire – www.crossfireinc.com
Custom Products – www.customproducts.us
Dye – www.dyeprecision.com
Empire – www.empirepaintball.com
End Game – www.endgameinc.com
Equation Design –www.equationusa.com
Evil – www.evil-paintball.com
Hammerhead – www.hammerheadpaintball.com
J&J Performance – www.jjperformance.com
JT USA – www.jtusa.com
Lapco – www.lapcodirect.com
Opsgear – www.opsgear.com
Palmers Pursuit Shop – www.palmer-pursuit.com
Planet Eclipse – www.planeteclipse.com
Pursuit Marketing Inc– www.pminetwork.com
Powerlyte – www.powerlyte.com
Proto Paintball – www.protopaintball.com
Psychoballistics – www.psychoballistics.com
Raven – www.ravenusa.com
Redz – www.redzcomfort.com
Sanchez Machine – www.sm1paintballbarrel.com
Site Manufacturing – www.sitemfg.com
Smartparts – www.smartparts.com
System X – www.systemx.com

Tippmann – www.tippmann.com
Titanium Paintball – www.ti-paintball.com
Viewloader – www.viewloader.com
Warped Sportz – www.warpedsportz.com
White Wolf Airsmithing – www.whitewolfairsmithing.com
Worr Games Products – www.worr.com

Clothing & Pads:

32 Degrees – www.32ice.com
Aci – www.airconcepts.com
Animal Paintball – www.animalpaintall.com
Blackstar Paintball – www.blackstarpaintball.com
Brass Eagle – www.brasseagle.com
Custom Sports Gear – www.customsportsgear.com
Diablo – www.diablodirect.com
Dye – www.dyeprecision.com
Empire – www.empirepaintball.com
Evil – www.evil-paintball.com
Extreme Rage – www.extremeragesports.com
Flurry Industries – www.flurryindustries.com
Game Face – www.gamefacepaintball.com
Hundreth Monkey – www.hundrethmonkeycaps.com
JT USA – www.jtusa.com
Kingman – www.kingmanusa.com
Mantis – www.mantisgear.com
Planet Eclipse – www.planeteclipse.com
Pursuit Marketing Inc – www.pmi.com
Proto – www.protopaintball.com
Raven – www.ravenusa.com
Reactive – www.reactivepaintball.com
Redz – www.redzcomfort.com
Ronin – www.ronin-gear.com
Smart Parts – www.smartparts.com

Special Ops – www.specops.com
System X – www.systemx.com
Tippmann – www.tippmann.com
Worr Games Products – www.worr.com
Wdp – www.wdp-paintball.com

Hoppers & Loaders:

Allen Paintball – www.allenpaintball.com
Avalon – www.diamondgt.com
Empire – www.empirepaintball.com
Extreme Rage – www.extremeragesports.com
Odyssey – www.odyssey.tv
Pursuit Marketing Inc – www.pminetwork.com
Ricochet – www.ricochet2k.com
Turbo – www.turbo-paintball.com
Viewloader – www.viewloader.com
Warped Sportz – www.warpedsportz.com
Zap – www.zappaintball.com

Markers:

Aka/lmp – www.akalmp.com
Aim Paintball – www.aimpaintball.com
Airgun Designs – www.airgun.com
Alien Paintball – www.alienpb.com
Ans – www.ansxtreme.com
Ariakon – www.ariakon.com
Bob Long – www.boblong.com
Brass Eagle – www.brasseagle.com
Bt Paintball – www.bentippmann.com
Chipley Custom Machine – www.chipleymachine.com
Component Concepts – www.phantomonline.com
Diablo – www.diablodirect.com

Dye – www.dyeprecision.com
Empire – www.empirepaintball.com
Evil – www.evil-paintball.com
Game Face – www.gamefacepaintball.com
Indian Creek – www.icdpaintball.com
JT USA – www.jtusa.com
Kingman – www.kingmanusa.com
Palmers Pursuit Shop – www.palmer-pursuit.com
Planet Eclipse – www.planeteclipse.com
Proto Paintball – www.protopaintball.com
Pursuit Marketing Inc – www.pminetwork.com
Shocktech – www.shocktechusa.com
Smartparts – www.smartparts.com
System X – www.systemx.com
Tippmann – www.tippmann.com
Viewloader – www.viewloader.com
Warped Sportz – www.warpedsportz.com
Wdp – www.wdp-paintball.com
Worr Games Products – www.worr.com

Masks:

Brass Eagle – www.brasseagle.com
Dye – www.dyeprecision.com
Empire – www.empirepaintball.com
Extreme Rage – www.extremeragesports.com
Game Face – www.gamefacepaintball.com
JT USA – www.jtusa.com
Kingman – www.kingmanusa.com
Pursuit Marketing Inc – www.pmi.com
Proto Paintball – www.protopaintball.com
Raven – www.ravenusa.com
Scott USA – www.scottusa.com
Vforce – www.vforcepaintball.com

Packs, Pouches, Vests:

32 Degrees – www.32ice.com
Aci – www.airconcepts.com
Allen Paintball – www.allenpaintball.com
Avalon – www.diamondgt.com
Blackstar Paintball – www.blackstarpaintball.com
Brass Eagle – www.brasseagle.com
Cops911 – www.cops911.com
Custom Products – www.customproducts.us
Dye – www.dyeprecision.com
Empire – www.empirepaintball.com
Era Paintball – www.erapaintball.com
Evil – www.evil-paintball.com
Extreme Rage – www.extremeragesports.com
Flurry Industries – www.flurryindustries.com
Game Face – www.gamefacepaintball.com
Gen X – www.genxglobalinc.com
JT USA – www.jtusa.com
Kingman – www.kingmanusa.com
Mantis – www.mantisgear.com
Nxe – www.nxepaintball.com
Opsgear – www.opsgear.com
Planet Eclipse – www.planeteclipse.com
Proto – www.protopaintball.com
R7 – www.r7usa.com
Raven – www.ravenusa.com
Redz – www.redzcomfort.com
Rhino – www.rhinotechusa.com
Ronin – www.ronin-gear.com
Smart Parts – www.smartparts.com
Special Ops – www.specopspaintball.com
Syndicate – www.syndicategear.com
System X – www.systemx.com

Viewloader – www.viewloader.com
Warrior Sports Gear – www.warriorsportsgear.com
Warsensor – www.warsensor.com
Worr Games Products – www.worr.com

Paintballs:

32 Degrees – www.32ice.com
Archon – www.archonpaintball.com
Arrow Precision – www.arrow-precision.com
Blue Arc – www.bluearcpaintball.com
Brass Eagle – www.brasseagle.com
Diablo – www.diablodirect.com
Draxxus – www.draxxus.com
Empire – www.empirepaintball.com
Evil – www.evil-paintball.com
Fuego – www.fuegopaintball.com
Game Face – www.gamefacepaintball.com
Great American Paintballs – www.greatamericanpaintballs.com
JT USA – www.jtusa.com
Jumbo – www.jumbopaintball.com
Karnage – www.karnagepaintballs.com
Nelson – www.nelsonpaintball.com
Pursuit Marketing Inc – www.pminetwork.com
Proto – www.protopaintball.com
Severe – www.severepaintball.com
System X – www.systemx.com
Tippmann – www.tippmann.com
Viewloader – www.viewloader.com
Worr Games Products – www.worr.com
Xo Industries – www.xoindustries.com
Xball – www.xnallpaintballs.com
Zap – www.zappaintball.com

ABOUT THE AUTHOR

Steve Davidson is considered one of the founding fathers of modern paintball. His experience with the game has involved virtually every aspect of the industry—from retail sales, to manufacturing, event promotion, authoring, lecturing, serving as an expert witness, designing innovative products, operating playing fields, officiating, team management, coaching, and being a general advocate for the sport.

In 1999, Steve was voted one of the "Top 100 Players of All Time" by *Paintball Games International Magazine*, one of the highlights of his 23+ years in the industry.

Steve has written two previous books about paintball—*Maxing: A Guide to Winning Tournament Play* (1994, Rabid Chihuahua Publications) and *The Complete Guide to Paintball* (2000, Hatherleigh Press) and has authored more than 200 regular monthly columns and feature articles for magazines such as *Paintball News, Action Pursuit Games, Paintball, PaintCheck, Paintball Sports, Paintball Games International* and *PaintMag*.

Steve founded the World Paintball Federation in 1990 and created the team scoring, seeding and ranking systems still in use today. In 1992, he founded the National Professional Paintball League and served as its coordinator from 1992 until 1994. In 1996 he was elected the NPPL's Secretary.

In 1997 he began work on creating a new paintball league specifically geared towards spectators and television broadcast. He received a patent for his game format in 1999, and introduced it in 2000 at the PaintFest event, the country's third largest tournament that year, which also incidentally hosted the nation's first National Collegiate Championships.

Steve recently took over as Editor-in-Chief of www.68Caliber.com, one of the industry's leading news and information websites. He continues to consult for select clients and participates in various paintball forums on the web. He is currently at work on a science fiction novel.